In Their Own Hands

How Savings Groups Are Revolutionizing Development

Jeffrey Ashe
With Kyla Jagger Neilan

16
EasyRead Large

ISBN: 9781459684140

RHYW

Copyright Page from the Original Book

In Their Own Hands

Berrett-Koehler Publishers, Inc.
235 Montgomery Street, Suite 650
San Francisco, California 94104-2916
Tel: (415) 288-0260, Fax: (415) 362-2512
www.bkconnection.com

Ordering information for print editions
Quantity sales. Special discounts are available on quantity purchases by corporations, associations, and others. For details, contact the "Special Sales Department" at the Berrett-Koehler address above.
Individual sales. Berrett-Koehler publications are available through most bookstores. They can also be ordered directly from Berrett-Koehler: Tel: (800) 929-2929; Fax: (802) 864-7626; www.bkconnection.com
Orders for college textbook/course adoption use. Please contact Berrett-Koehler: Tel: (800) 929-2929; Fax: (802) 864-7626.
Orders by U.S. trade bookstores and wholesalers. Please contact Ingram Publisher Services, Tel: (800) 509-4887; Fax: (800) 838-1149; E-mail: customer.service@ingrampublisherservices.com; or visit www.ingrampublisherservices.com/Ordering for details about electronic ordering.

First Edition
Paperback print edition ISBN 978-1-62656-218-9
PDF e-book ISBN 978-1-62656-219-6
IDPF e-book ISBN 978-1-62656-220-2

2014-1

Book design: VJB/Scribe. Copyeditor: John Pierce. Proofreader: Nancy Bell. Index: George Draffan. Map of savings groups in Mali courtesy of Oxfam America; Cartographer: Molly O'Halloran. Cover and color insert photos: Jeffrey Ashe. Photo of Jeffrey Ashe: Alyce Getler. Photo of Kyla Jagger Neilan: Jeff Fidget.

TABLE OF CONTENTS

The introduction of Saving for Change in a new community starts with the approval of the village authorities.

The first group is trained by an animator (in blue) from a partner NGO.

The volunteer replicating agent trains groups, with an illustrated manual to guide the discussion.

Each week members gather to save and borrow.

The box keeper takes the locked cashbox out of hiding and brings it to the group.

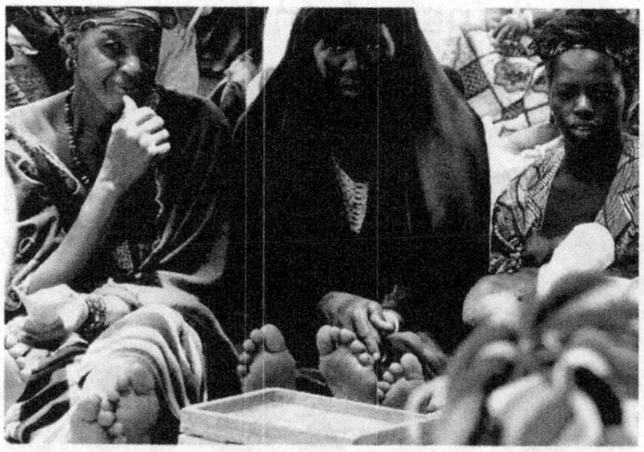

The group's officers open the meeting with a recitation of the bylaws.

Each woman in turn deposits her saving and repays the interest or principal on her loan.

At the end of the cycle, each member receives back all that she saved, plus her share of the interest.

Even with low literacy levels, group treasurers created a way of record keeping by placing pebbles in a small bag.

Carrying their wooden stools on their heads, women from one group walk to visit another.

Loans are used for many purposes. This woman used her loan to stock her business.

A collective enterprise set up in a Saving for Change group produces sambal, a nutritious sauce, in the city marketplace.

Two savings group members hug at a Saving for Change meeting in Senegal. Members often teach their daughters to run their own groups.

Women in Mali garden collectively and sell what they grow in the market. Their Saving for Change group helps them manage their resources through the seasons.

The man at the left, from an NGO in Cambodia, trains the group secretary to keep records.

Group trained in the prevention and treatment of malaria. The blue picture card shows the steps.

Saving for Change youth groups spring up spontaneously, even though fostering them was not part of the program. This group in Cambodia shows how important these groups are to their members.

Meetings are communal affairs, with children looking on and sometimes participating. A treasurer counts money while her daughter looks on.

Savings for Change groups often serve as platforms for other community initiatives. In Guatemala, the woman on the right successfully organized the groups in her region to campaign and vote for women mayors in their communities.

The secretary and the treasurer of a group in Guatemala keep track of the transactions in their groups.

A Saving for Change meeting is not only about saving and borrowing—it is also a chance to have fun. A Saving for hange member dances for her group in Mali.

More Praise for In Their Own Hands

"Jeff Ashe gives us one of his biggest dreams yet. People living in p overty organizing and using their own capital to provide the savings and credit that help them withstand shocks and take advantage of opportunity. What's more, Ashe and Neilan show us that this dream is being realized millions of times and spreading rapidly across the globe."

—Larry Reed-Director, Microcredit Summit Campaign

"Most books on community finance are either anthologies or manuals. This one is neither. A radical departure from other works in the field, *In Their Own Hands* traces the long sweep of financial empowerment via histories viewed through the single lens of one author. The book is essential for any practitioner interested in helping the poor transform small amounts of money into meaningful ways of changing their lives."

—Kim Wilson, Lecturer, International Business and Human Security, The Fletcher School of Law and Diplomacy, Tufts University

"Jeffrey Ashe and Kyla Neilan's new book, *In Their Own Hands,* presents a stunningly simple, thoroughly tested, and visionary new way for the poor to save and borrow. In Mali, the outcome was dramatic: less hunger, ownership of more livestock, and more clout for village women. The remarkable difference with savings groups is *how* they are able to achieve scale—not through building financial institutions as microfinance has done but by catalyzing the problem-solving capacity of the poor. The ideas in this book have the potential to turn the development field on its head."

—Paul Polak, coauthor of *The Business Solution to Poverty* and Chairman, Windhorse International

"I can think of two good reasons to read *In Their Own Hands.* One, if you give a damn about extreme poverty, here is another practical tool in the arsenal of financial inclusion. Two, amidst all the chatter about listening to and capturing the wisdom of impoverished communities and indigenous peoples, this book is a road map on how to do it. The author's economic development career reveals a professional courage from which we can all learn."

—Jonathan C. Lewis, founder and Chair, MCE Social Capital

"Since I met Jeff in Ecuador in the '60s, he's been turning conventional wisdom on its head. He does this now for the financial sector and for the development community grown too comfortable with in-the-box thinking. The title of the book says it all—*In Their Own Hands.* Those of us who want to help need to break from the past, trust the impoverished, and get out of the way so that they can empower themselves to save and be agents of their own development."

—John Hammock, former President, Accion International and Oxfam America

"I have known and admired Jeff Ashe for almost forty years. I consider him—along with Muhammad Yunus—one of the most innovative practitioners of the global microfinance movement. He was my principal mentor in developing the methodology of Village Banking. When in the year 2030 the world celebrates the end of severe poverty on our planet, Jeff's tireless efforts to promote rural savings groups will be heralded as the single most effective, bottom-up strategy for 'leaving nobody behind.' And for the next generation of microfinance practitioners, *In Their Own Hands* will be justly recognized as the best end-poverty textbook ever written."

—John Hatch, founder of FINCA International and cofounder of the Microcredit Summit

"Modern savings groups are an improvement on the self-help tools poor people have always used to manage their money. This short and clearly written book shows how over 100,000 villages in the developing world have come to use and value such groups and why it's important to spread the message to millions more."

—Stuart Rutherford, author of *The Poor and Their Money,* coauthor of *Portfolios of the Poor,* and founder of SafeSave

"Sometimes the most powerful ideas are the simplest. This book shows how a simple way for communities to accumulate savings has taken off—with no new technology nor costly microfinance infrastructure. *In Their Own Hands* turns upside down the most common assumptions about what poor households need and can accomplish."

—Jonathan Morduch, Professor of Public Policy and Economics, Robert F. Wagner Graduate School of Public Service, New York University

To Alyce, my wife and my life's companion; your love and support have meant the world to me.

Foreword: Frances Moore Lappé

Frances Moore Lappé is the cofounder of the Small Planet Institute and author of eighteen books, including *Diet for a Small Planet* and, most recently, *EcoMind: Changing the Way We Think, to Create the World We Want.*

I'll bet most of us wouldn't expect a book about savings groups in developing countries to shake up our ideas about the human condition and our sense of possibility for our world. I didn't—but that's just what this fascinating book has done for me.

My curiosity was first piqued in learning of the meteoric rise of savings groups: in the world's poorest countries, in just six years, membership in village-level savings groups has leaped from one million to ten million members. If there were a speed record among global social movements, the rise of savings groups may have broken it. Remarkably, much of this speed reflects the work of villagers voluntarily teaching other villagers, with only minimal donor help.

For several decades, I've been convinced that a primary cause of many of our worldwide problems in poverty and development is a lack of vision of what can work. Without a believable vision of where we want to go, we feel defeated and powerless.

That's serious. Since solutions to all our biggest problems, from poverty to climate change, are known or just around the corner, I've come to feel there's really just one problem we should be most worried about: the spreading sense of powerlessness to manifest what we already know.

In Their Own Hands helps me refocus my energies to this end.

Jeffrey Ashe appropriately warns us that, "joining a savings group will not lift many out of poverty." Savings groups are no panacea. What comes clear to me in this eye-opening book is that the movement indeed touches the taproot. In the people we meet in this book, I see the beginning of self-organizing power to meet three deep human needs: for connection, for meaning, and for power itself—power understood as our capacity to create and make an imprint.

Powerlessness means feeling vulnerable, dependent, and alone. Savings groups address each of these. They enable members to become more resilient in the face of poverty's assaults—as loans can be used not only to get you through a poor harvest but to purchase supplies for your small business or help if a family member develops malaria or HIV/AIDS. The groups build trusting connections as members create and enforce rules together, and they offer meaning as members enjoy the experience of directly helping one another succeed.

The stories you will read here bury the myth that poor people have too little to save, that expert staff must manage loans, and that financial independence begins with a loan. We learn what might have seemed obvious but apparently has not been: starting a self-help initiative with a loan, i.e. debt, increases one's sense of vulnerability. "Debt equals stress," Ashe reminds us. Starting with savings does the opposite.

If this book's message feels far from the lives of those in developed countries, think again. So many people in the North feel they are victims of a globalizing corporate banking elite, speeding the stream of wealth to the very top. In contrast, all the gains stay close to home in the simple system of savings groups. The control is with the village women, not with moneylenders or bankers.

I believe the qualities that define successful societies are distributed power, transparency in human relationships, and cultures of mutual accountability. Such characteristics make possible what I call "living democracies," everyday cultures of democracy that support life. What astonishes me, as I read *In Their Own Hands,* is that the savings group movement embodies each of these qualities. They are the "nano" versions.

Not many who write about revolutions have experienced one. Ashe's internal "rethink" of the microfinance system led directly to the writing of this book. For twenty years, Ashe explains, he worked in the microfinance movement where local people are not in control. After being a leader in a field for so long, few would have the courage to see, much less acknowledge, a better way and change course.

Ashe's core paradigm shift, which he loves to repeat with a smile, is "They know how." Most aid interventions collapse as soon as outsiders leave, he notes, but the savings group approach transfers some very basic tools and gets out of the way. It enables people to tap into their own ingenuity, determination, and creativity. So it lasts, and it spreads.

"We are on the verge of a revolution in development, where savings groups are just the starting point," Ashe writes. He could be right. Revolutions aren't necessarily noisy, in-your-face disturbances. This quiet and virtually invisible one begins on the inside, and its premise and practice are so incredibly simple that one could easily miss its power. Reading this book, you will not run that risk.

Preface: Ray Offenheiser

Ray Offenheiser is the president of Oxfam America.

When Jeffrey Ashe joined Oxfam America ten years ago, I admit that I had reservations about how his savings group model would sit with Oxfam's rights-based approach to development and our strategic goals. But I recognized the approach as an innovative one, and it was an idea with strong potential to be scaled up. And anything that builds the resilience of women and men living in poverty aligns with Oxfam's mission. So Jeff joined us.

Sometimes it pays to take a chance. I am proud that we at Oxfam took that risk with Jeff.

Saving for Change is one of the most successful development innovations I have witnessed in my career. It turns the traditional notion of microcredit on its head by allowing group members to save before they borrow. The premise of Saving for Change is that the poor are not too poor to save but are instead too poor *not to save.* When neighbors save a few cents together each week, not only do they gain access to basic financial services, but they also build social capital on a foundation of trust and solidarity.

Today, savings groups are reinventing themselves. The byproducts of savings have proven to be every bit as valuable as the savings themselves. Gains in social capital, self-confidence, and women's empowerment translate into health and maternity clinics, grain banks, markets, and thousands of thriving small businesses.

Savings groups have unexpectedly created a channel for delivering other benefits to members. Participants drive this process. At their request, Oxfam has used groups as an educational forum, offering training on topics such as business, citizenship, and agriculture in addition to our basic training module. Saving for Change has also become part of a larger effort at Oxfam: our Rural Resilience Initiative—a partnership to innovate and develop better tools to help vulnerable farmers mitigate the risks and consequences of climate change so that they can earn a living and support their families.

What is perhaps most striking about Saving for Change is how it seems to strengthen the capacity of individual village-level savings groups to solve problems: to identify what their communities need, to organize themselves, and to seek solutions independent of aid organizations such as Oxfam. People are learning more about their ability to help themselves. In Mali, women concerned that the nearest health clinic was too far away used their group funds to build a clinic—right there in the village. They convinced each family to contribute one hundred bricks for building and used their newly acquired influence to gain the mayor's support. In Africa and Central America, savings groups are coming together in local associations to hold authorities accountable, ensuring that local government officials honor their development promises. In Senegal, eight women decided to represent their communities by seeking seats on local mining councils. They report that they would never have considered such a role had they not become participants in Saving for Change.

There are countless similar stories. Even the simplest is remarkable, because each traces how the seemingly mundane creation of a savings group can change the lives of dozens—sometimes hundreds, even thousands—of women, children, and men. The task of choosing whose stories to tell must not have been an easy one. But Jeff did just that. Sifting through years of research, rich experiences, and his notebooks, he carefully selected stories that allow the reader to meet the women and men who accompanied him on his journey and are changing the world every day.

When I consider the benefits of Saving for Change—the money saved and loaned, the financial gains, the increase in social capital—I think often of a woman I met in Mali. She was walking to her savings group meeting, a small hand-carved foot stool balanced on her head scarf. The change these women are creating in their lives is impressive, and their business meetings are often infused with an unmistakable air of celebration. What she told me gave me a glimpse of the incalculable benefits that members accrue: "When you miss a meeting," she explained, "you miss the best party of your life."

They certainly have reason to celebrate.

INTRODUCTION

Beginning a Savings Revolution—They Know How

Two and a half billion people worldwide, most of them in desperately poor, rural communities, need a better way to save and borrow. The overarching and hopeful message of *In Their Own Hands* is that improving financial services for the poor need not be complicated or expensive if responsibility is firmly in the hands of those who directly benefit. Local ownership and control is the essence of "in their own hands" development. As local communities take charge of the financial aspects of their lives, they gain the skills, confidence, and motivation to do more. In the words of Marcia Odell, who taught me that savings groups were possible in Nepal more than a decade ago, "Dependency is not empowering."

In Their Own Hands is a book about learning to be courageous, to take risks, and to make change happen. Rather than critiquing development, *In Their Own Hands* provides clear guidelines for how to develop and carry out initiatives that work.

This is a book for those who are already working for change abroad and at home, seeking a better way to do development that avoids dependency and helps achieve transformative change. Foundations and agencies funding grassroots efforts can use this book as a reference to refocus their efforts away from funding handouts and toward empowering the poor to take responsibility for their own change.

In addition, this book is for anyone who is curious about what it takes to make a difference. Educators will find this book useful as they introduce students to the effort it takes to implement effective grassroots development and the courage and dedication it takes to achieve it.

Savings Groups: Turning Banking on Its Head

Savings groups are a robust, simple, game-changing financial innovation that reaches the village poor by turning banking on its head. Instead of attempting to extend the reach of financial institutions that cannot profitably reach the poor, small groups of community members are trained to manage their own mini-financial institutions. Members save what they can weekly in a communal pot and loan their growing funds to members. Annually, timed for when money is scarcest, the pot is divided according to how much each member saved plus each member's share of the interest. Every cent saved over the cycle plus interest is returned to the members. As a woman in Nepal I interviewed said, "Why pay them when we can pay ourselves?"

The simple model of savings groups is a marked difference from traditional financial institutions—banks, microfinance providers, large credit unions—with their imposing buildings, armies of staff, and complex systems, which rarely reach these rural areas. The principal reason why membership in savings groups has grown from one million to ten million in just six years is that instead of depending on institutions, savings groups tap into the vast, underutilized potential of smart people to solve their own problems.

Through the discipline of weekly saving, community members now have a useful sum of money in hand when cash is scarcest. With their end-of-year payout, they buy food during the "lean season," before the harvest puts food on the table. They may pay school fees, purchase medicine, stock a business, grow more food, or buy a goat or two to fatten and sell. Benefits are not only financial; now that members have their own money to spend, women (most of the group members are women) have gained a measure of independence and benefit from the growing solidarity and mutual assistance among members.

Savings groups are as convenient as meeting under a tree in a village and as flexible as the rules members design for themselves. They are as reliable as their own accounting, which is quite dependable if registers are simple and training is adequate. They are easy for villagers to understand because they build on how women have saved for generations. "These savings groups are like a *tontine* [West African traditional rotating savings group], only better," a woman in Senegal once told me. Instead of working like a traditional *tontine,* with each member in turn receiving her payout of the total collected that meeting, a member of a savings group can take out a loan when and in the amount she wants, as she saves the amount of money she can. Interest is charged on the loans, and fines are levied when members miss meetings or do not pay a loan on time, so when the fund is divided, members receive more money than they saved. More flexibility comes at a cost: the need for better record keeping. Better record keeping is the focus of savings group training and the major task of the local nongovernmental organization (NGO) staff who train these groups.

In the decades that I have been involved in promoting change, I have observed that savings groups are the best example of the power that local ownership and control can have. Savings groups overcome the risks of top-down efforts to improve the lives of the poor. What outsiders create often fails when they leave; what villagers create through *their* efforts persists, evolves, and grows. It follows, then, that our task as outside agents is not to *provide* services, but to catalyze *the capacity of poor communities to resolve their own problems.* After working to promote this type of approach to development for decades, I've identified nine principles needed for success:

- Start small to learn, but plan for scale—if there are thousands of communities, what will have been achieved if only a few are reached?
- Simple is better than complex.
- Build on what is already in place and already widely understood.
- Design for change that persists long after outside agents leave and that spreads from village to village without outside staff.
- Keep costs low: resources are scarce and the scale of poverty is vast.
- Give nothing away: if what is introduced depends on a free handout, it will not spread.
- Insist on local control: if local community members are in charge, new development initiatives will last.
- Establish high performance standards and insist on meeting them.
- Build learning and innovation into program design: it is impossible to get it right the first time.

These principles are described in greater detail in chapter 1.

By adhering to these principles, the number of savings groups could grow fivefold or even tenfold in a decade, from a hundred thousand villages to a million villages. Assuming that savings group membership grows from ten million today to fifty million by 2020, these groups will by then mobilize and largely distribute US$1.25 billion of their own money every year, of which $750 million will be profits from lending. This growth is impressive especially considering that the individuals who are mobilizing resources at this scale are among the poorest people in the world, whose annual income is often less than $500 a year. The poor are not too poor to save.

These lessons of savings group promotion can be applied across the development spectrum, including areas such as agriculture, health, enterprise development, business literacy, education, and advocacy, among others. This task is already underway with promising, scalable results, described in chapter 7.

A savings-based approach will become increasingly necessary as the poorest countries and poorest regions cope with increasing challenges of climate change, scarce and depleted land, and endemic conflict. Given the amount of development assistance that is misspent and the declining amount of aid to the poorest countries overall, the value of a simple, replicable, and sustainable approach can hardly be overestimated. "In their own hands" development works—it builds resilience, reduces chronic hunger, and increases assets. (The impact of membership in a savings group is described in chapter 6.) Although much more is needed—basic infrastructure, markets, government services, good governance, more equitable division of resources—savings groups are a reliably useful starting point.

A Call to Action

Savings groups work. It is time now for the development community, including foundations and bilateral and international agencies, to get behind the expansion of the savings group model. While microfinance works well in the densely populated villages of Bangladesh and in cities and their surrounding communities, it is often not the best answer in scattered rural villages. In countries marked with political strife, collapsing economies, and unchecked inflation, not only do savings groups work, but they work where microfinance fails.

The systems and the institutional capacity are already in place to accomplish this.

The cost for training and supporting savings groups is extraordinarily low. Each group creates its loan fund through weekly savings and tracks its own payments. Securing loan capital, tracking transactions, and ensuring that loans are repaid are the major costs of financial institutions. Once the groups are trained, except for an occasional monitoring visit, they manage themselves. The groups do most of the work—selecting members, electing officers, deciding on their bylaws, creating their own loan fund, deciding who will receive a loan, and making sure loans are repaid.

Compared with what is spent for development every year—US$44.6 billion in 2010 alone for the fifty-four least developed countries[1]—the $150 million per year needed to bring savings groups to fifty million participants over seven years is inexpensive indeed. An investment of about $1,500 in each village, spread over three years, will predictably lead to a decrease in chronic hunger, an increase in assets, and an increase in social capital. If the average village size is about one thousand people, *this works out to $1.50 per person.* And this is only the start: in the fourth, fifth, and sixth years after groups have been trained, I have seen that the groups grow in size, that they save and invest more, and that they launch their own initiatives—training groups for their children, buying grain when the price is low to better survive the lean season, and launching collective enterprises as they reach out to other NGO and development programs. With their economic clout, management skills, and group solidarity, they aspire to more.

I have come to realize that "in their own hands" development may be one of the very few viable paths for jump-starting development in the million or so villages of the world's poorest countries, so why is funding so difficult to secure? Despite the obvious benefits, funding the training of savings groups does not easily fit into the way development is usually carried out. There are scant opportunities for investors. There are no massive development institutions with their thousands of workers and few well-told stories collected by journalist staff to delight and impress donors in order to loosen up their purse strings. In this "neighbors talking to each other" development model, the electronic gizmos that so delight Silicon Valley millionaires are not front and center, although villagers may call each other on their cell phones to organize a meeting. What has occurred is more subtle, but ultimately more profound: villagers are in charge and they follow their own agenda.

What savings group practitioners call the "savings group revolution" is remarkable in that it is almost invisible—a group of people in a rural community sitting under a tree put money in a box, with a few of them taking money out of the box as loans to attend to urgent needs. Each group has what it needs to survive, to grow, to evolve, and to self-replicate. Savings groups may just be the most effective use of a "smart subsidy" on record, where so many positive benefits can be achieved at such a small cost. Once the basic structure of the savings group model is introduced to a rural community by an outside agency—usually a local nonprofit—the groups do virtually everything, including training more groups.

What is needed are the will and the resources to achieve the benefits that expanding the outreach of savings groups would provide. This small investment would not only provide a safe and convenient place to save and easy access to small loans, but it would enable savings groups to help slow, or potentially even reverse, an increasing spiral into debt for the world's poor. Savings groups can also serve as a launching pad for development initiatives that communities undertake on their own and sometimes with the help of a local nonprofit or government program.

The Savings Group Movement

Oxfam America, Freedom from Hunger, CARE, Catholic Relief Services (CRS), Plan International, the Aga Khan Foundation, Pact, and many other international and local organizations have made the promotion of savings groups a central tenet of their development strategies. Today, there are savings groups with ten million members living in at least a hundred thousand villages in sixty-five countries. Six years ago, there were just one million savings group members. As Frances Moore Lappé describes in the foreword, the growth in savings group membership must have set a speed record. I know of no other development initiative that has grown so quickly and in so many countries that shows the broad applicability of this methodology across nations, cultures, and religions.

In 1971, Moira Eknes and her team at CARE developed the first savings groups in a remote corner of Niger. It was only decades later, in 2008, that a major investment by the Bill & Melinda Gates Foundation helped spur rapid growth in the field, attracting more funders, including MasterCard Foundation, USAID (the US government's development agency), and the Inter-American Development Bank, as well as high net worth individuals and a number of smaller foundations.

This massive scale-up has been achieved not through building financial institutions, as microfinance has done, or by transacting finance in the cloud, as mobile banking is doing now, but by catalyzing the problem-solving capacity of the poor to lead their own development, with a little transitory support from an outside agency. Paying the local staff to train groups is virtually the only expense other than research, the training of trainers, advocacy, and developing new products.

Although savings groups are uniquely designed to effectively reach the world's poorest, they aren't able to address every financial need in these areas. Both microfinance and mobile money have a unique role to play in expanding financial inclusion. Savings groups are most appropriate for the rural or urban poor, who need a place to save more than they need a loan and are beyond the reach of financial institutions. Microfinance is best suited for those with a business large enough to benefit from a loan and in areas where there is more economic activity. Members of savings groups whose needs are greater than the group can finance often take out loans from financial institutions.

Between 1980 and today, microfinance has grown from a few scattered projects carried out by NGOs to two hundred million borrowers today. Credit unions reach a similar number. Mobile money facilitates remittances from workers in the city to their relatives in the villages and extends the reach of financial institutions. Everyone can work together to provide financial inclusion for the two and a half billion who need a better way to save and borrow. If nonprofits introduce this improved way to manage finances that savings groups represent in a scattering of villages throughout a region, we may learn that new savings groups have sprung up spontaneously to fill in the gaps between groups that were trained by paid staff.

In Their Own Hands: Empowerment as Development

In Their Own Hands is the story of how I came to see the impact of savings groups—once I learned how they worked, I never turned back. This book is about how we can learn from the power of savings groups and apply the principles I learned over years of working in this field to move development forward.

Before I learned about savings groups, I had designed, managed, and evaluated microfinance institutions for twenty years. While microfinance was working well in urban areas, I concluded that it was not serving the rural poor. I built from what I learned in Nepal, and later in India and Zimbabwe, to launch and lead the Oxfam America/Freedom from Hunger Saving for Change initiative that has, since 2005, trained and supported savings groups with 650,000 women members in thousands of villages across Mali, Senegal, Cambodia, El Salvador, and Guatemala.

Through this experience, I have learned that the poor are not too poor to save, that there is enough savings potential within a group of twenty people to meet most needs within a small community, and that small sums can make a big difference. Once groups have mastered the mechanics of savings and lending, they begin to ask, "What's next?" With a reserve of savings and the knowledge that they can easily access small loans to meet an immediate need, they gradually come to believe tomorrow can be different from today. The disciplined hard work of saving every week and running a group has made a difference.

FROM MICROFINANCE TO MICROSAVINGS: A PERSONAL JOURNEY

I have worked in microfinance almost from its inception in the early 1980s, working to create and evaluate microfinance institutions (MFIs) in thirty-five countries, including the United States. Through my position at Acción International, I joined the movement to create a "best practice" model of microfinance project design: large-scale, well-managed, permanent financial institutions that provide credit (and sometimes savings and other services) to those not reached by traditional banks.

As I continued to design microfinance projects in eastern Europe, Africa, Asia, and Latin America, I began to look closely at the different self-managed savings and lending clubs that poor people around the world used to meet their basic financial needs. People joined *zadrugas* in Bosnia, *equibs* in Ethiopia and Eritrea, *tandas* in Mexico, *cadenas* in Colombia, *tontine* s in West Africa, *chit funds* in India, *merrygo-rounds* in East Africa, and *partners* in Jamaica. These are only a few of the hundreds of variations of what are technically referred to as Rotating Savings and Credit Associations (ROSCAs). In *The Poor and Their Money,* Stuart Rutherford and Sukhwinder Arora call this process "the world's most efficient and cheapest financial intermediary device" because "at each round the savings of many are transformed instantaneously, with no middlemen and no transaction costs, into lump sums for one person."[2]

As the 1990s went on, I continued designing and evaluating microfinance programs, but I kept returning to a fundamental question: Why do we start with microloans (i.e., microdebt) and not savings? Wouldn't the security of savings be better than the stress of repaying a loan? Poor borrowers, I could see, often used their high-interest microfinance debt for consumption and emergencies instead of investing in profitable businesses that could pay their loans' interest. These borrowers struggled to repay. I saw that debt often equals stress.

Then, in 2000, I heard Marcia Odell, then the director of Pact's Women's Empowerment Program in Nepal, give a speech at Brandeis University. It forever changed my understanding of microfinance. I learned that savings-led microfinance was not only possible but was already being implemented in Nepal. The Women's Empowerment Program (WEP) worked through savings and lending groups, whose members mobilized their own savings and made loans to one another. I traveled to Nepal three times to document the model, which led me to evaluate similar initiatives in India and Zimbabwe over the next two years. These programs, even though they were developed independently and were not aware of each other, were organized on the same principles—the groups saved to build a loan fund, loans were made from the growing fund as members needed them, and the groups distributed the profits from lending to the members. *There was no link to a financial institution or any injection of outside capital into the group fund.*

Understanding how these programs worked became an obsession of mine. These savings-led initiatives had remarkable success, reaching poor villagers, most of them women, at low cost and on a large scale, with the profits from loans paid to the group members. Savings groups start with savings—building assets rather than debt. Trained groups of community members, not financial institutions, manage transactions.

SAVING FOR CHANGE

In late 2004, I was hired to introduce savings groups to Oxfam America's Community Finance Department as the department's director. I worked hard to ensure that Oxfam's version of "community finance" reached populations that financial institutions, even the most innovative microfinance institutions, had scarcely touched. Saving for Change, our name for this model, was designed to support Oxfam's work to "right the wrongs of poverty, hunger, and injustice." Oxfam's focus is on the world's poorest communities, with an approach to work through local partner organizations. My colleagues and I at Oxfam, along with Kathleen Stack and her colleagues at Freedom from Hunger, another advocate for self-help solutions to end hunger, developed Saving for Change. Saving for Change capitalized on the unique skills of local nonprofits (NGOs): outreach, training, and hands-on support. This program set local grassroots nonprofits at the heart of our design and built on what they already did so well: delivering services and training in poor and often remote villages.

Our mission was to develop a locally controlled, easily accessible, scalable approach to improving financial inclusion to reach a population that microfinance as it is traditionally conceived never will. No money can be made on weekly savings deposits of twenty-five cents and fifty dollar loans, the scale of the transactions that the poor most often need. We calculated that in Mali alone, a country with a population of nearly sixteen million,[3] the potential market for savings group membership was substantially greater than one million members, just counting women, who were the target for Saving for Change membership. We chose to target women because Saving for Change was more than just a better way to save and borrow—we wanted to provide opportunities for women to develop their organizational and leadership skills in a forum where they could discuss issues of importance to them.

Eight years later, nearly 450,000 women had joined Saving for Change groups in Mali, in addition to the 143,000 villagers in Mali who had joined similar projects sponsored by CARE, the 40,000 who were part of Plan International projects, and the 30,000 who had joined groups trained by CRS. By early 2014, a total of 695,589 savings group members were trained in Mali among the four organizations.[4] To put this in perspective, this figure is larger than the entire population of Boston, and it puts savings group membership in Mali into the top ranks of microfinance outreach worldwide—this was financial inclusion without financial institutions.

Speaking just of the Saving for Change part of this expansion into Mali, we achieved this level of outreach (450,000) with a staff that never exceeded 203 people. This included a staff of trainers (animators) and their supervisors working for ten local NGOs and a team of four Malians who made up the technical unit. The number of staff working with groups is now one-third of that number, with virtually no sign that the groups are faltering. The groups were taught to manage themselves and to share what they had learned, and so they did. While the ratio of staff to borrowers is typically 1 to 300 for a financial institution, the ratio for Saving for Change in Mali was 1 to 2,000 during the high-growth stage. Since village volunteers increasingly took the lead for training and supporting groups, this ratio has grown to about six thousand group members for every NGO staff person.

Savings groups are hardly a perfect solution, and some groups function better than others. One limitation is that the amount that each group can save and distribute each year is small—about $500 in countries like Mali—so loan size is limited. Another limitation is that it takes a lot of time and effort to meet every week. Members do not seem to mind in the dry season, when there is more time and a savings group meeting is the perfect excuse to get together, but time is limited when the rains come and all are busy in the fields. There is also always the chance that someone with higher status will have an easier time getting a loan.

With that said, 95 percent of the groups trained in Mali since 2005 continue today. Despite these problems, groups have been able to resolve their difficulties, and they keep coming back week after week and year after year.

Joining a savings group will not lift many out of poverty—no development initiative can deliver on that promise—but regular savings and a reserve of cash can help reduce life's uncertainties.

ASSESSING THE PERFORMANCE OF SAVING FOR CHANGE IN MALI

In 2006, the local Saving for Change team in Mali—including representatives from Oxfam America, Freedom from Hunger, and the Strømme Foundation, our donor and collaborator in identifying initial partners—and I carried out the first assessment of Saving for Change. This assessment was a chance to see how—and if—Saving for Change actually worked for its members. I had managed and evaluated dozens of programs before, but it is different when you are checking on your own initiative, especially when it is new and unorthodox. I felt a little nervous as the plane touched down in Bamako, Mali's capital.

Mali, one of the poorest countries in the world, is a landlocked country in West Africa, with its northern half firmly planted in the Sahara Desert, and its southern part, where we implemented the Saving for Change training, in the semiarid Sahel. The team climbed into a program vehicle, left Bamako, and drove through a flat plateau of scrub grasses dotted with intermittent, colossal baobab trees. We left the main road and veered sharply onto a rutted, rocky dirt track. Two hours later, we came upon the cluster of mud houses that marked the first village stop on our ten-day assessment trip.

We exchanged appropriate greetings with village leaders and staff of the local NGO (trained by the Oxfam America and Freedom from Hunger team),[5] and then the savings group meeting began. I followed along as best I could, knowing the general order of business and receiving a few helpful whispered translations from Mariame Coulibaly, a local Saving for Change staffer who worked for the Strømme Foundation.

The women repeated their bylaws in unison, as they did every week. The officers took attendance, opened the cashbox, and reported the total to the members—it had to be the same as when the box was closed at the end of the last meeting, ensuring that no transactions occurred during the week. Once the women had each contributed their savings and earlier loans from the fund were repaid, the secretary announced the new total in the cashbox. The group president then asked if anyone wanted to request a loan. A few placed one of their sandals in front of them or raised their hands to indicate they did, and a lively discussion ensued, with the borrowers explaining how the loans would be used and the rest of the group debating the likelihood they would be repaid. By the end of the meeting, most of money in the box was loaned out.

As the discussion wrapped up, the trainer from the local NGO carrying out Saving for Change in this region, the "animator," led us to a meal prepared by one of the groups. I assumed we would be getting back into the car to head to the next village after lunch, but instead the animator brought us to watch another group meeting in another part of the village. When that meeting finished, she had us wait to attend a third, and then a fourth. As another efficiently run Saving for Change meeting unfolded before me, I was concerned. Had the animator we had contracted with through the local NGO to seed savings groups in twenty nearby villages merely stayed put, thoroughly organizing this one place at the expense of all the others?

It turned out that this village had eleven Saving for Change groups, with a combined membership of about 250 women. It was an impressive number. I interrupted a conversation transpiring in Bambara between the Malian staff and the animator before she took us to sit through another meeting. She assured me that she had indeed trained groups in surrounding villages, as she had been expected to do. In fact, the animator had organized only one group in this village. The rest of the groups were trained by Salimata Coulibaly.

Salimata, or Sali, was the president of the first Saving for Change group in the village. Unlike most of the women there, Sali attended school up to the eighth grade. She ran a small kiosk selling necessities such as matches, salt, sugar, and tea. Sali was small, lean, and intense. She wore glasses and a tightly tied *hijab* wrapped around her face, which contrasted with the flowing scarves and head wraps that most other women wore. Sali was all business. I had been impressed with how smoothly she directed her group. I was more impressed as I realized that she had cultivated that same impeccable order in ten more.

"How did you do it?" I asked Sali through a translator. She explained that it was not so difficult; she simply repeated each weekly lesson the animator taught her group as it formed, reviewing with ten other groups how to choose members, elect officers, craft bylaws, and keep records. Sali would meet with each of the ten groups she organized in turn and pass on what she had learned.

"Why did you do it?" I asked. A year later a group making a video that featured Sali asked her this same question. She answered:

> I want better development for my village. The women trust me a lot. That's why they always come to me for advice. It is with great joy that I share my knowledge with them. I would like to have this program reach everyone. There are some villages that have not been reached. I would really, really want to have these women receive the learning we have received.[6]

During that first assessment, Sali took us to task, saying we needed to do a better job teaching the women to keep records. Since most of the women in her groups were illiterate, Sali explained, they ask their husbands to step in and handle record keeping. Sali declared, "Sooner or later, the men will steal from us."[7] We took this request to heart and later introduced a record-keeping system based entirely on oral recall so that groups without a single literate member could keep their own records.

The groups Sali Coulibaly organized were, to my eye, equal to those groups created by the animator, a trained and paid NGO staff member. I began to believe that even at this early stage we were on the right track. Our vision was that some group members would volunteer to train new groups in their villages within two years, as I had seen elsewhere. Having volunteers train and support the groups is the cornerstone of both controlling costs and ensuring that the groups continue beyond the scope of the project. The volunteers live in the village, but the paid staff will soon go on to another village. Within months after the first group was formed in her village, Sali was training new groups with no special guidance or training from Saving for Change.

If Sali had taken it upon herself to organize groups in her village, perhaps other leaders were training groups in their villages. I asked her supervisor what the animator team had told him about groups replicating spontaneously. He said that while Sali was unique in the number of groups she had trained, he knew of several other volunteer replicators who had each already trained a group or two. The next day, in a new village a half-day's drive away, Fatoumata Traoré, an animator from another local NGO, reported that she too knew of many villages where group leaders were training groups.

Nine years later, we know that of the 18,700 groups in place in Mali today, volunteers trained well over half of them. We now incorporate volunteers, whom we came to call "replicating agents," as an integral part of our strategy. What emerged on its own in a few villages that first year with a little extra training and encouragement (and no payment), we were able to duplicate in thousands of villages.

Sali Coulibaly saw something in Saving for Change that inspired her to teach the idea to her peers. Her story was emblematic of the underlying ethos we tried to build into Saving for Change: ownership. Each group was managed by its members, using their own money to build assets collectively that they could access throughout the year in the form of loans. Annually, dividends that included their year-long savings and the interest garnered from the loans were distributed back to the members. Our theory was that if members owned and operated the groups, members could adapt their groups to fit their specific financial needs. We hoped this would lead members to value the groups as a resource so much that they would decide to share their knowledge with others. Sali manifested this hope tenfold.

The savings group practitioners, operating quietly in the rural backwaters of the world's poorest countries, are demonstrating that what is needed is a disciplined commitment to savings.

Savings groups are not the end point, only a beginning. We are on the verge of a savings group revolution.

CHAPTER 1

Guiding Principles for Saving for Change

After years of promoting savings groups, I have identified nine principles that explain why the number of savings groups has grown so quickly, how they have replicated organically, and why these groups survive in the face of economic and political crises, armed insurgencies, drought, and hyperinflation. These same principles could be applied to any development initiative attempting to reach not just hundreds but thousands—even millions—of people at minimum cost in a way that is robust enough to continue long after outside staffing and funding has ended.

Start With a Vision of Scale, and Design for Viral Replication

Sir Fazle Hasan Abed, the founder of Bangladesh-based BRAC, the world's largest NGO, said, "Small is beautiful, but big is necessary." Every rural community is unique, but our task was to build a "good enough" intervention that could be duplicated widely. The sign of a well-implemented good idea is that others adopt it as their own. In Mali, well over half of the groups currently in place were trained by volunteers. Recall the conversation with Sali Coulibaly.

Less Is More, and the Simpler the Better

The key is to introduce a new idea and get out of the way as soon as those you are assisting can do it themselves. With too many visits and too much help, the groups remain dependent. My team developed a solution that met villagers' needs and was to be run by women in rural communities who had little or no formal schooling. For them, sticks, seeds, and pebbles were used to quickly tally outstanding loans, a system that proved to be far more accurate than written records. Simplicity translates into scale, low cost, and the spread of ideas by word of mouth.

Build on What Is Already in Place

Savings groups improve on traditional revolving savings groups—ROSCAs—which are already widely understood in the communities where we work. While savings groups and ROSCAs share the requirement that groups select their members, save regularly, and hold each other accountable, savings groups add variable savings, taking out loans when and in the amounts desired, improved record keeping, charging interest on small loans, and greater transparency. I knew we were on the right track when, after a few minutes of describing Saving for Change to a woman in Senegal, she responded, "I understand how this works. It's like a *tontine,* only better."

Be Sustainable

While many development programs have no lasting impact, approximately 95 percent of the Saving for Change groups in Mali, some of them trained almost ten years ago, are still saving and lending. Most are visited only every few months or not at all. While operating independently, these groups have survived a coup, an insurgency in the north, a major drought, skyrocketing food prices, influxes of displaced people, and faltering institutions, so there is little reason to believe they will weaken in the future.

Keep Costs Low

There are never enough resources. For an initiative to grow quickly and organically, costs must be low. For Saving for Change in Mali, support totaled $1,500 per village, which included training several groups and then progressively less frequent monitoring over three years. The documented impact justifies the modest cost—a decrease in chronic hunger, increased assets, more savings, reaching the poorest, and word-of-mouth replication within the village and neighboring villages as volunteers from established groups trained groups on their own account.

No Giveaways

Dependency kills innovation and restricts the viral spread of ideas. Alfred Hamadziripi, the Zimbabwean director of the CARE Village Savings and Loan Association (VSLA) program, told me of the disastrous first months of the program in his country. Each group received a matching grant equivalent to the amount they saved. The groups saved, received the match, and disbanded. Their motivation was to receive a handout, not the disciplined business of mobilizing and managing their own savings. CARE dropped the matching requirement in Zimbabwe, and the number of groups soared. In Saving for Change, the "no-giveaway" rule also means that groups pay for accounting forms and cashboxes. If there are no giveaways, those who choose to join groups fully recognize that the eventual success (or failure) of the venture is entirely in their own hands.

Insist on Local Control

Garnering local ownership can be a challenge, but it is a necessity. Local control allows the community to drive instead of only being along for the ride. The genius of savings group programs is that they can be carried out by local NGOs that devolve the responsibility for training more groups to volunteers. If groups depend on the presence of an outside staff person, they will disband when the outsider leaves.

Establish High Performance Standards and Insist on Meeting These Standards

Meeting high performance standards must matter in development work as much as it does in the business world. Know the targets that you want to reach and ensure that you get there. For example, each team of ten paid animators and a supervisor is tasked to introduce Saving for Change to three hundred villages with a combined population of three hundred thousand inhabitants. There were clear objectives for each team and each paid staff person. Each team was required to facilitate the training of eight hundred groups, of which two hundred were trained by the staff—one per village—and the remaining six hundred were trained by volunteer replicating agents who would train and support more groups after the staff was reassigned to another cluster of villages. Once objectives are clear, achieving them is much easier.

Embrace Learning and Innovation

Allowing for local control and respecting community input means constant improvement. Innovations from one village can spread only if the model is flexible and everyone involved is committed to learning. Using the principles of appreciative inquiry, NGO staff were periodically brought together and went through an exercise in which they were asked to define success in specific terms—a growing savings rate, excellent record keeping, and high attendance at meetings, among others. They were asked to rate how well the groups they were working with were meeting these objectives and then to come up with a plan for improving performance in any areas that lagged. Finally, to bridge the gap between planning and action, staff members were asked to commit to a specific action when they got on their motorcycles the next day to start to resolve this issue and to specify how success would be measured.

These principles are remarkably simple. In essence, each reflects the title of this book: *In Their Own Hands: How Savings Groups Are Revolutionizing Development.* If we truly believe that "they know how" and that our presence is to serve as a transitory catalyst of change, then the rest follows—scale, simplicity, building on what is there, sustainability, low cost, no giveaways, local control, setting standards, and embracing learning. I believe that this is the surest path to reaching the more than two billion people who could benefit and underpins my assertion that improving the lives of the poor need not be as complicated and costly as we once feared.

CHAPTER 2

A Group Meeting

The following tale of a savings group meeting is a sketch drawn from many sources. The village Kouloukoura and its economy, environment, and social structures were crafted from a composite of villages in its region that have been closely studied by Oxfam America, Freedom from Hunger, Innovations for Poverty Action, and the University of Arizona's Bureau of Applied Research in Anthropology. The characters featured here are themselves composite sketches, drawn from case studies of and interviews with savings group members and data that indicates what a typical group in this area may look like, including its members' livelihoods, family structures, and finances.

Kouloukoura

Bintou was thinking about rain as she wiped sweat off her forehead and put down the short hoe she used for weeding. Hours before noon, the day was already hot. Bintou lives in Kouloukoura, Mali, a midsize village of a few thousand people located in Mali's expansive Koulikoro region. The region is tucked below the Sahara desert to the north, where agriculture gives way to cattle herding. Kouloukoura, like many of Mali's villages south of the desert, receives enough rainfall for villagers to cultivate many crops; the size of the harvest, though, is extremely vulnerable to the impacts of seasonal rains and drought.

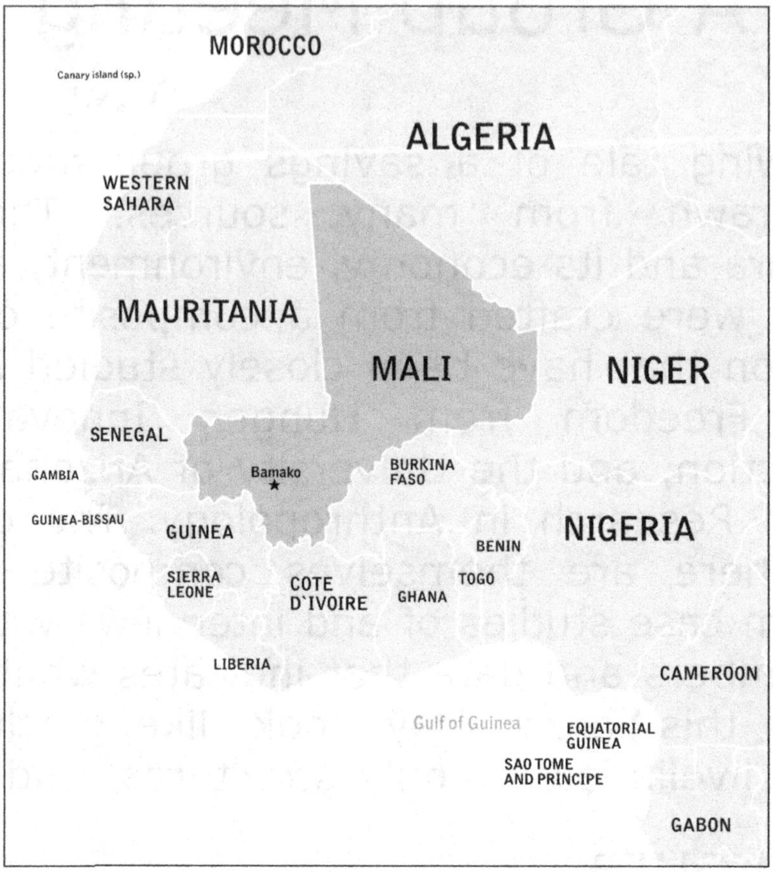

Location of Mali in Africa

Bintou was eager to cut short her time in the field to attend her Saving for Change meeting, even if it meant forgoing an hour or two of work she could do before the sun got unbearable. She hadn't seen some of the women in her group since the last meeting and was excited for the chance to catch up. She made one last sweeping glance over her fruiting tomato plants before bending down to hoist a wicker basket onto her head, overflowing with peanuts she'd brought out of storage earlier that morning. She walked briskly down a well-trampled path of off-white, hard sand, glancing across the small cornfields and tight stands of trees near her home.

As she walked, Bintou poked her head in the entryways of neighbors busy inside the low walls of their household yards. Each wall surrounded an open-air living space bordered by a few mud houses with thatched or tin roofs, round thatched granaries, and shoulder-high, open-roofed latrines and bathing rooms. Some of the yards had small gardens like Bintou's within their walls or just outside. Most were bustling with little kids and three generations of women cooking over pots perched on stones, over coals fueled by firewood the women had collected earlier. Other women pounded millet in big wooden mortars with heavy four-foot-long pestles. In one yard, two teenagers were throwing the pestles into the air and seeing how many times they could clap their hands before catching the mortar as it fell. The rhythmic knock of the mortar provided a steady beat under everyone else's movements.

At this time of morning, most men were out tending their corn and millet fields, while the women were up and about, finishing chores before heading out to the fields to join their husbands. Of course, they still had time to pause and ask after Bintou's health and that of her family as she went by.

A Savings Group Meeting

Bintou was one of the last to arrive at the mango tree where the meeting was held, so she quickly found her place in the circle of twenty-one women and sat down among the group, emptying the basket of peanuts in front of her. Some other women in the group were also shelling peanuts, while others held their young children. Everyone sat on *pagnes,* colorful, multifunctional cloth wraps that serve as skirts and wraparound baby carriers. Bintou leaned over to grasp hands and say hello to her friends and then pulled a handful of peanuts out of the pile and began to shell them, dropping the raw, hulled nuts back into her basket.

The group was sitting in the center of the village, the mango tree casting just enough shade to make the meeting pleasant as the hot morning sun climbed into the sky. With everyone settled, Aminata, the group's president, raised her voice to ask the first question. "Is everyone here?" she said in Bambara, the dominant language in the region, turning to the person on her right. Each woman made the same motion, confirming that the person who always sat next to her was indeed there. "What is our group called?" she sang out. The group replied, *"Benkadi,"* meaning solidarity.[1] Aminata continued through the group's opening process, a ritual that laid out the agreed-upon ground rules and expectations at every meeting. Restating the rules upfront tended to keep disagreements and confusion to a minimum, especially since the group had no written charter, which could alienate members who could not read.

"What is our goal?" President Aminata asked.

The members called back, "To divide what we have saved all year among ourselves."

"How much do we save each week? What is the fine for not saving? What is the fine for missing a meeting?" Aminata continued, pausing after each question for the group's reply. When the group had stated aloud the terms for loans they had agreed to and a reminder of the meeting time and place, the president called for the collection of savings.

Oral Accounting

Three women stood up. One held a key aloft as she stepped to the middle of the circle, while another bent down to pick up a metal box by her feet and brought it to the first. The president asked the group to announce the amount of money that should be in the box: 14,400 of the West African franc, abbreviated CFA (US$30).[2] The two women unlocked the box and placed it down so that the third woman could count the money. There was respectful silence while she worked. She announced, "14,400CFA." The first two women sat back in their places while the third, the cashier, remained with the box.

Next, the president asked to collect the fines owed from the last meeting for absences, tardiness, missing a savings deposit, and late loan payments. Failing to bring one's savings deposit meant having to pay a 50CFA fine (10 cents) the next week in addition to bringing both weeks' savings. Being late cost another 25CFA and an absence cost 50CFA (5 and 10 cents, respectively) unless the member sent along her savings and a good excuse with another member.

A few women raised their hands and in turn called out the fine owed by the woman sitting to their immediate right. Group members always sat in the same order, so each person could act as a "helper" for the one next to her. When the president called the name of a woman who owed money, the woman stood, occasionally to the ribbing of her fellow group members if she was one of those who teased back. The group was serious about money but easy on each other. They repeated the amount of their fines and handed it to the cashier, who announced the payment to the group fund. Hearing each step made every member a participant in the accounting, ensuring that everyone could follow along and understand.[3]

After the fines came the savings. While most women saved a single share of 100CFA ($0.20) per week, many committed at the beginning of the yearlong savings cycle to bringing two, three, or up to five times that amount. When the fund was divided, those who saved more would receive two to five times the dividend of a woman who saved only one share. When it was her turn, Bintou stepped to the cashier and placed 200CFA—two shares—in the palm of the cashier, who counted it and placed it in the box. She sat back down and grabbed another handful of peanuts.

Collecting savings and fees was the last part of the short weekly meetings, which usually dissolved into an impromptu party before everyone had to head back to work. Once a month the group held an extended meeting for paying old loans and taking out new ones and for hosting topical discussions and trainings. This was one of those longer meetings. Each member with an outstanding loan paid the interest on her loan, 100CFA for every 1,000CFA borrowed, or 10 percent per month. They decided to charge each other this high interest rate so that they could build the loan fund more quickly and receive a larger payout when the fund was divided. Once the interest was paid, those whose loans were due that meeting repaid them in full. Most of the loans were small, under twenty dollars; fifty dollars would be considered a large loan for the group. The majority of women repaid within one month, although some loans were for two or three months, and agricultural loans extended over as many as six months. After loan business concluded, the cashier counted and announced the amounts of savings, fines, and loans collected and the new total in the cashbox—26,000CFA (about US$53). This was how much they could lend out this meeting.

Requesting Loans

The president then asked whether anyone would like to take a loan. Three women raised their hands, including Bintou. President Aminata called on her to speak first. Bintou pushed aside the pile of peanuts at her feet and stepped around her basket to stand in the center of the circle. She explained to the group that she needed a loan of 5,000CFA to buy smoked fish and onions here in Kouloukoura to sell at the big weekly market in Soma. For the past year she'd sold these in Soma along with bags of roasted peanuts. With the loan, she could purchase more stock and expand the business. It had been a loan from her Saving for Change group that had allowed Bintou to begin selling in the Soma market last year.

The president thanked Bintou and asked for the next person to speak. Kadija stepped to the middle of the circle. This was the first time Kadija approached the group for a loan; she had been too afraid of the interest charges to ever take one before. She joined the savings group to build a savings account and to take advantage of the interest garnered from the loans of others. She had joined also to handle emergencies such as she faced today.

Kadija explained to the group that her husband was very ill, stuck in bed with a fever. He had not been able to work in their millet field for more than a week and had missed a chance to sell a goat at the Soma market. The family was running low on rice and millet stores, and Kadija didn't have cash to buy more. She requested an emergency loan to buy a bag of grain, to be paid back when her husband recovered. Kadija valued her privacy and her pride, so she hesitated to bring her family's needs up for group discussion, but she appreciated her ability to do so. Her savings group was more discreet and reliable than asking her family or, worse, begging or going without.[4]

Several women responded with blessings and murmurs of good wishes for her husband's recovery. Aminata spoke up, telling Kadija that *Benkadi* did not charge interest for loans in emergencies, and borrowers could pay the loan back at their own pace.[5] The members of *Benkadi* prioritized emergency loans for helping members in need.[6] Group members earned access to this safety net when each week they tightened their already narrow budgets and skimmed a few cents off their regular household purchases, depositing the money in the group fund. The effort other members put into gathering their savings validated each other's economic struggles, while the buffer their savings and loans created to deal with risks like these motivated each to save more.[7]

Finally, Tabika explain her loan request. Tabika was one of the busier merchants of the group, supported by two sons in Bamako and a husband with steady income as a nurse at a community health center in a nearby village. Her youngest child, barely a year old, was wrapped in a *pagne* tied as a sling around her torso, resting his head drowsily on her shoulder. Tabika saved four shares in her Saving for Change group and regularly took out loans. She said her son was visiting from Bamako soon and she would like a two-month loan of 20,000CFA ($40) to give him money to buy children's clothes, which she would sell here and in Soma. Tabika already had an outstanding loan from a few weeks earlier for buying sweet potatoes to sell as French fries. She said the new loan would not interfere with paying back the first loan because she would separate them to make record keeping easier. She had begun taking overlapping loans very early in the savings cycle and had always paid on time.

LOAN 1: SUPPORTING A STRUGGLING BUSINESS

When everyone who wanted to take out a loan had finished explaining her needs, President Aminata opened each request to discussion in turn. She began again with Bintou. Bintou stood in the middle of the circle, listening to the discussion going on around her. Occasionally the group decided not to lend to someone or to ask a member to come to the next meeting with a revised plan more likely to result in timely payback. Other times they had to offer loans smaller than requested, depending on the amount of money available in the group fund at the time. Since it was their own savings that they were lending, the group was understandably cautious. That said, the members generally wanted to make loans because the loans would be repaid with interest. The more loans they make that are successfully repaid, the more money they accrue at the end of the savings cycle.

Bintou hoped her previous experience selling in the market would convince her fellow group members that she could easily make enough profits to pay back the loan and its interest, as well as earn a profit for herself and her family. One woman in particular disagreed. Assiatou argued that Bintou had missed her savings contributions at least once before, at the end of the lean season last year, before her family's harvest had come in. She wondered aloud how well Bintou fit her business—including the long walk to and from the Soma market—around all her household chores, agricultural labor, and childcare, as the season wore on.

Another woman responded to Aminata. Fanta was well respected because of her age and because she was the oldest woman in her large extended family, which included her husband and six children, a younger co-wife and her four children, and her husband's two younger brothers, their wives, and their children. Like Tabika, one of her sons worked in Bamako and her husband earned a regular salary, working as a schoolteacher, so her family had more money and was more educated than most in the village. She managed that household and her own garden and found time to cook and sell hot meals outside her home most evenings, stocking up on ingredients with regular loans from her savings group, where she saved five shares per week. Fanta's opinion mattered, so when Fanta told the group that she'd seen Bintou sell out of her wares in the Soma market before, those who had been skeptical eased off. In the savings group, personal relationships replaced collateral as assurance that borrowers would repay their loans. Those who trusted Fanta believed in Bintou. Since Fanta was already well respected in the group, her endorsement meant a lot to the other members.

At this point President Aminata stood and asked the group's members whether they thought Bintou should get her loan. A chorus of *"Awo,"* yes in Bambara, went up, and Aminata looked pointedly at those who had expressed disagreement earlier. Assiatou and a few others nodded yes.

LOAN 2: EMERGENCY FOOD CRISIS

Aminata brought Kadija's request to the group. For the savings group, giving emergency loans to members in need filled many with pride. They could provide financial support to their friends and neighbors when what each could give individually would not have been enough. Kadija's loan request received no opposition. Instead, a few women who knew Kadija's family offered to bring a few bowlfuls of millet to her home before the market, to ensure that the family had enough to eat.

Kadija thanked everyone for her fortune to receive such generosity. Silently, she worried about repaying the kindness because, unlike Bintou and others in the group, Kadija rarely made or grew enough of anything to sell. Often she barely managed to make the weekly savings contribution, a few times struggling to pay fines for late payments on top of the regular deposits. She had skipped a meal that day and was tired from working in her family's farm plot without her husband's help over the past few days. She sat down heavily, grateful, tired, and already running the math in her head. With millet to make it to market day, she could buy enough grain with the loan to feed her family for another few weeks. She prayed that would be enough time for her husband to get better. Her family often ran out of food toward the end of the *soudure* dry season, just before harvest, but this was early, and it did not bode well for the leanest period.[8] She wondered whether she would need to sell one of her husband's goats herself and whether he would let her.

LOAN 3: SUCCESSFUL BUSINESS

Finally, Tabika stood up, the child tied to her back now awake and playing with her hair. Immediately, someone brought up Tabika's outstanding loan. This didn't faze her, and Tabika waited for a following speaker to remind the group that all year Tabika had loans that overlapped and had always paid them back on time. There had been one occasion several months ago when Tabika's youngest child, barely an infant at the time, was sick with malaria. She had spent most of her loan money on medications and then become ill herself, unable to buy the ingredients to prepare the meals she sold. Even then, Tabika's husband had stepped in and given her money to make her regular payment.[9] Besides being grateful to his wife and for her ability to access the money they needed to care for their infant, Tabika's husband wanted to be sure that she remained in good standing with her savings group because it had taken on such an important role in their family's budget.

With a good record and visible, profitable businesses providing assurance, the group did not need to discuss Tabika's request for long before agreeing to it.

Tabika thanked the group and sat down, conducting mental calculations of her own. Though her enterprises were some of the most successful of the group, Tabika's trading had plateaued. She spent her loans on purchasing stock to trade, but her profits were constantly redirected to consumption needs for herself and her family. She was stuck in a pattern of taking out repeated loans to sustain the same activities as when she first joined her group.[10]

At the same time, while Tabika's economic growth had stalled in the short term, she knew her savings and loans had enabled her to make economic decisions from a stable foundation upon which a better livelihood could be built—she could plan ahead knowing she had access to loans now and a share-out coming at the end of the year. This stability had a noticeable effect. Households in rural Mali operate in a climate of extreme and chronic vulnerability; unforeseen calamities such as malaria or drought regularly undermine planning for the long term. Perhaps over time, Tabika might be able to absorb greater risk and reinvest more and more of her earnings into a bigger business.

Loan Disbursements

Aminata announced the names of the three women receiving loans. Each walked toward the cashier, who announced the amount as she handed the money over. She calculated the 10 percent monthly interest on the loan, to be paid each month until the end of the loan, when the principal is due. Bintou pledged the amount aloud to the group: "I am taking a loan of 7,500CFA for one month. I am going to pay the loan and 750CFA in interest at the loan meeting next month." Bintou's helper repeated the message, committing it to memory.

The other borrowers went through the same process, though Kadija's loan had no interest and it was understood that her payback date could be extended if need be. It was expected that she would do her best to pay back the loan before the group's annual share-out. At the share-out, they would collect all outstanding loans and disburse the entire sum, including savings, interest, fines, and earnings from collective income-generating projects such as working as a group on a neighbor's field for a day.

Once the loans were handed out, the cashier recounted the money left in the box and announced the total. Everyone joined hands and repeated the number together before the cashbox was closed and locked by Aminata. The money management portion of the meeting was over.

Malaria Education

At this point a woman seated across the circle from President Aminata stood up.[11] Djeneba had been quietly watching the group's interactions. Djeneba was the group's animator, the staff member of a local NGO who had arrived in Kouloukoura the previous year tasked with forming a Saving for Change group if the community was interested. She had spent the meeting reflecting on when she first organized these women into *Benkadi.* She had led introductory meetings with community leaders and later with villagers to explain the savings group idea, ask questions about the community's financial practices and needs, and gauge enthusiasm for forming a group.

The members of *Benkadi* were the women who had been most excited to try out the new group saving idea. Many were slightly better off or more socially connected in the village, better positioned to risk trying the new idea.[12] Most had already pooled money together before in smaller cash "merrygo-round" groups called *tontines,* the traditional rotating savings associations common in Malian villages. In a *tontine,* members contribute a set amount of money to a pool that goes home with a different member in turn at each meeting. The simple mechanism enables its members to gather a usefully large sum of money for major purchases such as school fees or business investments, while requiring only small contributions at a time—particularly useful where members lack safe places to store growing cash savings and where the options for credit are nonexistent or perceived as usurious.

The Saving for Change idea sounded to them like an improvement on the basic *tontine,* turning weekly contributions into interest-garnering savings and allowing for flexible loan requests in different amounts and timeframes, a major difference from the rigidity of the *tontine* schedule. Importantly, the Saving for Change model still kept all money management within the group. Unlike the microfinance institutions that some households turned to, Saving for Change groups brought in no outside money. The interest on loans stayed with the group members, and no external collector would come to threaten a member who couldn't pay. Unlike the microfinance institutions, too, Saving for Change had protections built in to ensure transparency through oral record keeping, so all of the members understood the group's processes and finances, keeping everyone engaged and in control. Regular meetings reminded people to save each week.

The familiarity of the group with its members helped ensure that loans were repaid—and it left enough flexibility that the group could respond to emergencies, as it had for Kadija today.

The animator, Djeneba, remembered how exciting it had been when she started training groups. For the first six months of their weekly meetings, she led them through discussions so that they could decide on their responsibilities as members and come up with group rules guiding interest rates and fines. They set a collective goal (to divide their group fund, which would have grown larger from interest collected over the year) and elected a president, key holders, and a cashbox keeper. During this planning time, they were regularly saving their shares, so by the second month of meetings they had saved enough capital to begin lending. The first loans were a big relief to the cashbox holder, who immediately saw the benefit of disbursing the savings into the hands of members, diversifying the responsibility for protecting the money (and generating interest income too, of course).

After a few months of weekly savings meetings and monthly lending meetings, the group handled more and more of the process itself, with Djeneba receding into the background. The key to group survival would rest on the animator's ability to ensure that group members had confidence in themselves and the motivation to make the group work so that it could continue to operate without her.[13] After six months, Djeneba reduced her visits to every other week, and after nine months, the group rarely had any need to look to her for help solving a question, so she visited just for the monthly extended loan meetings.

Now, a year later, the meetings seemed to run themselves. Djeneba usually visited only quarterly, when she recorded data about the group for her NGO, a Malian nonprofit that collected records on its Saving for Change groups for Oxfam America, which oversaw the overall program. The compiled data helped Oxfam America monitor the group's progress and improve the program over time. Right now, though, Djeneba was halfway through a three-month additional training program for the group, a seven-session malaria prevention course. Malaria is a primary cause of death in young children in Mali and a leading cause of illness and its resulting loss of labor and income for all Malians.[14] Many a group member's business dream had been diverted when a malaria emergency forced a borrower like Tabika to spend loan capital on medicines or when exhaustion from the illness prevented a woman from implementing her plans. Most group members had survived the deaths of siblings or children. Because of the disease's impact on their lives, many savings group members already had a strong understanding of malaria, but they welcomed the informed explanations from the NGO-trained animator.

After greeting the women, Djeneba launched into her training on malaria prevention, following a curriculum developed by Freedom from Hunger, Oxfam's partner in Saving for Change. Instead of lecturing, she used the facilitation skills she'd practiced to generate dialogue. Djeneba encouraged the women to brainstorm and discuss ideas, allowing them to use their own judgment to evaluate why something like an insecticide-treated bed net would help protect from malaria-causing mosquitoes. Djeneba added that better nutrition and prenatal care could help make pregnant women, infants, and children stronger and more able to survive a bout of malaria, though not prevent it. She stepped in to dispel myths, such as that eating certain foods repelled mosquitoes. She asked the women what preventive tactics they used now and why.

"Is prevention better than treatment? Does the medicine always work? Can you always afford the medicine?" she asked the women, putting each question up for debate. "Who is most at risk for malaria?" Djeneba reminded them that infants and young children are most likely to die from malaria and that pregnant women who get infected are also at risk for anemia, low birth weight, or difficult births. Her goal was not to force everyone to always use bed nets but to ensure that the women learned enough to make educated choices about malaria prevention and treatment.

As she wrapped up, she told them that next month she'd discuss how to treat a bed net with insecticide so that they could do it at home, which is cheaper than buying a pretreated net. Djeneba thanked the women for their engagement and let them know she would stay after the meeting if anyone wanted to talk to her.

Replicating Agent Training

The training session concluded. President Aminata stood up once more. She thanked the members for coming to the meeting and reminded them of the time and location of next week's meeting. The women broke up into little groups, chatting, while a few with pressing tasks hurried home. The women who had brought things to work on, like Bintou had her peanuts, gathered up baskets or tied cloths into bundles, squatting down to hoist heavy loads on top of their heads.

Djeneba stepped away from a conversation with President Aminata to catch Bintou as she left the mango tree. Bintou put a hand up to steady the peanut basket as she turned back, curious and a little nervous—she had been awarded a lot of loan money that afternoon. What if the group had made a mistake and Djeneba was about to correct it?

Djeneba instead launched into a proposal.[15] She had just attended a "training for trainers" course taught by her NGO. They had asked animators like her to find Saving for Change members who had the dedication, open-mindedness, and passion to organize more women in their villages into Saving for Change groups and teach the skills to run their meetings themselves. She asked Bintou if she would like to train new groups in her village. Would Bintou like to become a replicating agent?

Bintou asked what the work entailed. Djeneba explained that if she agreed, they would go together to speak with Bintou's husband and get his agreement too before moving forward. Then Bintou would be invited to a three-day training with other replicating agents, where she would learn the process of organizing a group. She would receive a picture-based manual that leads replicating agents step by step through the process of forming a group.

Many women in Bintou's village had already approached Djeneba about forming them into a new Saving for Change group. As a replicating agent, Bintou would take on this task—she would help the women form a group, go over the steps of a meeting, and guide them to set their rules. Then she would attend their meetings as Djeneba did for *Benkadi,* helping members practice the steps, intervening less and less as the members learned to run the group themselves.

Bintou thought for a moment, considering the suggestion. Her small business had grown since she started selling vegetables with her first loan last year. With the added money from the business and share-outs, her family was eating better, even during the lean seasons when her family's grain storage was used up. With that first loan, Bintou found she could focus on increasing the yield in her garden by purchasing fertilizer and that she could afford the cost of travel to the bigger market to develop her trading business. Bintou had noticed a transformative difference in her life as loans and share-outs allowed her new business to grow. She still felt as though she worked all the time, but her labor had been paying off lately. Bintou knew she could spare a few hours per week to help other women in her village experience the same changes in their lives.

Djeneba emphasized that while animators may have technical knowledge, replicating agents come from the communities they organize, so they have a deeper knowledge of their neighbors' circumstances and needs. Djeneba explained that replicating agents are volunteers—Bintou wouldn't be paid—but her fellow villagers would respect her for this work. For some other replicating agents, newly trained groups had even volunteered a day of labor in the agent's garden to thank her and keep her motivated. This was an important role.

Bintou nodded slowly. Saving for Change was important to her. Members gained the ability to meet some of their families' endless immediate needs, smoothing the harshest valleys of their variable incomes; at the same time, many like Bintou could begin to save enough money to invest in a business, one that could someday be profitable enough to substantially alter their living conditions. Bintou could see that through these weekly savings and loans for small businesses, the group helped its members be better off. Emergency loans helped them weather illness and disaster, so they could avoid selling precious assets such as livestock or expensive farm equipment when circumstances might otherwise have forced them to sell livestock, or a plow, or a donkey-pulled cart. The changes in Bintou's life and the lives of her fellow group members were small, but they were significant. Life was less stressful now.

She agreed with Djeneba to go speak with her husband. She liked the idea of spreading this idea, helping to form savings groups.

CHAPTER 3

"Dependency Is Not Empowering"

It was the year 2000, and I was attending a microfinance conference at Brandeis University. After I gave my talk about a program in Burkina Faso that I had just evaluated, Marcia Odell, at the time the director of Pact's Women's Empowerment Program (WEP) in Nepal, walked up to the podium, and with a voice filled with passion told of a dramatically different approach to financial services for the poor. Pact's WEP initiative made it possible for small groups of village women to pool regular savings into a usefully large fund they managed themselves. They could borrow from that growing fund as they needed. A better way to save and borrow was being delivered in a simple, low-cost, replicable, and (as I was to learn later) self-replicating package. Marcia's talk was the beginning of my journey of transformation from microcredit to microsavings, and I never looked back.

I felt compelled to evaluate Marcia's program to better understand its approach and impact. One hundred and thirty thousand women saving and borrowing in a year—how was this possible? I pulled all the networking strings I could, and with support from

Pact, USAID, [1] and Freedom from Hunger, I finally secured the funding I needed. I had been a consultant to Freedom from Hunger for years, and they, like me, were interested in savings. Lisa Parrott, Freedom from Hunger's technical advisor in microfinance, also joined me in conducting an evaluation of WEP's savings group model in Nepal. Lisa and I visited Nepal three times, devoting a year of our lives to learning about and critically understanding savings groups. I had found my calling.

Pact's Women's Empowerment Program in Nepal

We first arrived in Katmandu during the monsoon. Driving out from the city to the lowlands on the border with India, we watched out the window of the car as we descended down treacherous Himalayan roads into the open wetland valley—Nepal's Terai region and its thousands of villages. Our process was simple. Pact's senior leadership in Nepal introduced us to the local NGO staff that directly trained villages on the savings group model. We visited WEP groups each day, and Lisa and I, with one or two of Pact's staff to translate, observed the WEP groups' regular meetings. After the meetings, Lisa and I spoke with the groups and asked questions.

We interviewed two to three groups per day, in school buildings, on porches, or in courtyards of houses of better-off group members or community leaders. Each night, Lisa and I and the small WEP team traveling with us reviewed what we learned over sweet buffalo-milk tea, momos, and dal. From these visits, we learned the basic process group members used to collect savings, ask for loans, and record transactions. Sometimes we dropped into villages by surprise and pulled together meetings to ensure that we did not just see the preselected, cherry-picked groups. It was encouraging that these groups also worked quite well and operated by the same principles.

These were the basics: WEP was organizing women into several twenty-person groups in each village. In total, more than 130,000 women joined 6,500WEP groups in little more than a year.[2] This achievement was extraordinary in itself, as no microfinance program I had heard of over the previous two decades had grown so quickly. The program grew so fast because it did not need to build a financial institution to provide loans; instead, it built on preexisting literacy and forest conservation groups—even microcredit groups. Each WEP group was a miniature financial institution in which the money loaned out came directly from members' weekly contributions to their savings accounts, and where the profits from borrowers' interest returned to and increased the size of the savings account of each member. Unlike credit unions, which often have hundreds or even thousands of members and are regulated to protect member savings, WEP groups operated informally under the regulatory radar. Transparency and self-management took the place of regulation. Regulation was not necessary; members observed every savings deposit and loan payment and discussed and approved every loan at their weekly meetings.

The members of the savings groups were careful because they were managing their own money. There were neither matching funds or handouts nor a link to an external credit source. "Dependency is not empowering," Marcia told us on our arrival, a mantra that she repeated with equal fervor every time we met. Group members purchased the lockboxes where they stored their money between meetings, the forms they used to keep their records—even the kerosene they used for the lanterns for their evening literacy classes. Instead of waiting for a handout, they took charge. Because they were in charge, the program grew quickly.

WEP had opened a new market for financial inclusion. Few of the almost entirely illiterate and impoverished members of the WEP groups had ever thought of taking out a loan from an MFI. They had no assets for a guarantee or any business to invest in, yet they were saving and borrowing. The few women we met who had previously taken out loans from MFIs now saved and borrowed only through their groups. "Why pay them," one woman said, "when we can pay ourselves."

As I learned more, Marcia's logic began to make sense. Every four months the groups distributed dividends to their members based on the profits from lending. Members explained to us how borrowing from their groups built their savings—even if it took a while to obtain a loan or if the loan might be smaller than they wanted because the amount they could borrow was naturally limited by the tiny amounts each group member saved. They were willing to wait.

While interacting with groups composed of some of Nepal's most marginalized women, Lisa and I noticed a pattern. At the beginning of every meeting, each person introduced herself. In recently formed groups, some members could barely muster the courage to stand up and stammer their names before sitting down to cover their heads in embarrassment, not wanting to speak in front of outsiders such as ourselves. By contrast, in groups that were a year old or more, the women not only introduced themselves proudly, they also eagerly answered our questions, and not just the group leaders but regular members chimed in as well.

WEP was about more than saving and lending—it was called the "Women's Empowerment Program" for a reason. Sometimes, even before receiving the specialized training on women's legal rights provided to many groups by the Asia Foundation, members leveraged their savings groups into advocacy groups.[3] We learned about groups coming together to work against partner abuse, alcoholism, and child marriage in their communities. Marcia recalled how it was common in the Terai region for human traffickers to recruit young girls by offering poor mothers money to send their daughters to "waitressing jobs," which were really brothels in India. Their daughters were their last remaining asset. Nepalese girls were in high demand by traffickers since they would be easier to control in a foreign country where they could not speak the language. WEP groups became a platform from which women rallied against the exploitation of their children by human traffickers. They told me they felt more courageous now that they were organized.

One image remains vivid in my mind. Lisa and I were talking to a group of women in southern Nepal, a village so close to the Indian border that we could see it. Members were telling us what had by then become a common refrain: with their WEP group, the women had their own money, so their husbands showed them more respect. They had joined with other groups to advocate against child marriages. Meanwhile, through a gap in the high adobe wall, I could see that a group of men was meeting on the other side. Through our translator, I learned that the village imam was exhorting the men to keep their wives subservient and under control. Two group meetings, two different agendas. The WEP groups appeared to be giving women more say in their households and as community-level advocates for women and children, but they faced considerable resistance.

Literacy was another pillar of the WEP program—in fact, it was the program's foundation. Pact had promoted literacy in Nepal for many years, providing literacy training through more than a thousand local NGOs. Pact used simple, well-crafted workbooks that taught new readers important information or skills while they learned to read. For WEP groups, the literacy workbooks taught members how to organize their group and how to keep records. Additional workbooks explained human and civil rights and how to run a business. Costs for literacy training were minimal because the instructors were local volunteers trained and supported by WEP's NGO partners. These committed volunteers met with their groups four evenings per week. The women studied and chanted the words in the workbooks, and as they learned to read, they learned the practical and the transformative messages the workbooks contained.

Saving and lending plus advocacy and literacy training made for a powerful program. However, it was something that I learned entirely by accident that brought to my attention just how important these groups were for their members. One of the group leaders mentioned that she had trained another group. Lisa and I were intrigued. Wasn't it the NGO's responsibility to train new groups? Why did she do it? The group leader told us she wanted to share what she had learned. In a village we visited a few days later, another leader proudly showed me her dog-eared WEP manual. "I trained twenty-one groups using that manual," I remember her saying. Voluntary replication became a central theme of our questioning.

At the end of our first tour in Nepal, we brought together group leaders to answer some final questions about WEP, focused especially on their particular role in training others in the method. We learned that compared with the structured way that WEP staff trained groups, the member-leaders' approach could hardly be more informal. Often, a few women from their village would approach a group leader, curious about what the group was doing. The leader would invite them to attend a meeting. On leaving the meeting, she would tell the women to round up fifteen or so others interested in saving and lending, and if they could pull together a group, she would train them.

I asked the leaders, "Since so many of you are already training groups, why not make a business out of it?" The immediate response was "No!"—almost in unison from all fifty women. One continued: "We would not be trusted; our motivations would be suspect. We train groups because women are asking for our help. How could we refuse them?" Later, when it came time to design a community finance program for Oxfam America, I would remember how much these women valued their savings groups. They inspired me to build the training of member-trainers into the design of Saving for Change.

WEP provided an answer to my growing uncertainty about how microfinance could reach villagers in numbers that could make a difference: not with loans that are often too big to manage and even more difficult to repay, but with financial services that meet the needs of village women. This was effective financing for women in scattered villages where financial institutions are weak and money is scarce, but it was also something more—a member-managed, member-owned model that spread through the enthusiasm of its local leaders.

Why did it work? Lisa and I reflected on this question after many days of research in Nepal. The answer was as simple as it was profound: WEP had abandoned the costly infrastructure that MFIs use to deliver loans—all the staff it takes to secure capital, make loans, collect on them, and prevent fraud. Due to the complexity of managing a loan fund, a typical MFI has, on average, one staff person for every 284 outstanding loans.[4] The task of the WEP staff and the 250 some NGO partners with which WEP collaborated was much simpler: to train groups until they could operate on their own. Once a group mastered record keeping, the paid staff could focus on WEP's literacy and empowerment agenda and move on to train more groups, whereas bank and MFI staff had to spend time making loans and tracking payments for as long as the group borrowed. Besides requiring fewer staff and for a shorter duration than an MFI, a model that transferred management to the group members introduced another important difference between WEP groups and institutional microfinance. Success became defined in terms of sustainability of the groups instead of the long-term survival and growth of the financial institutions—the locus of success was at the level of the member, not the organization.

WEP was based on the assumption that groups quickly learn how to manage themselves if asked the right questions. They called their training "appreciative inquiry," an area in which Mac Odell, Marcia's husband, was expert. Appreciative inquiry posed questions such as "What do you like best?" "What would 'better' look like?" "How could you achieve that?" "What will you do first?" "When?" "Who is responsible?" "How will you know that this has been achieved?" By the end of the appreciative inquiry, the women were already taking their first steps for putting their plans into action. Promoting savings groups is about training a few strong groups (the "positive deviants") that will become a good example for future replication.

Where did it fall short? While WEP was overall quite inspirational, several practical aspects of its implementation showed room for improvement:

- Dare to be simple: a simpler record-keeping system and a simpler curriculum for training for women's rights. One group had boiled down the curriculum developed by lawyers into a brief pamphlet with a woman holding an upraised fist on the cover.
- Build on what is there: capitalizing on the desire for women to train each other.

- Better accountability: selecting stronger local NGO partners and holding them more accountable for performance.

We built these insights into the design of Saving for Change.

As Lisa and I interviewed group after group in the sweltering Terai heat, each conversation shattered another of the myths underpinning microfinance program design—myths such as that the poor cannot save and that groups need expert staff to manage loans and that financial independence must begin with a loan.

In my eyes, microfinance had become too complicated, too rigid, too expensive, and too staff-intensive to effectively reach the rural poor. WEP provided a simple but effective alternative.

Marcia's Story

We traveled back to Katmandu and met Marcia, full of questions about her WEP program design and the decisions that went into it. As we discussed the program details with her, we learned that many of WEP's most creative aspects were the result of innovations that Marcia, Achyut Hari Aryal (WEP's microfinance specialist), and many others on Marcia's staff had developed when presented with obstacles by those who doubted she could accomplish what she set out to do. Like many innovators, Marcia had to take a leap of faith that what she proposed would actually work; she also needed to trust in her colleagues to carry it out.

In 1998, Pact received a $5 million grant from USAID to form microfinance groups. Marcia, as the project's field director, decided they could use Pact's existing literacy and other community-based groups to act as a platform for the microfinance project by introducing and linking these existing groups to external credit. Her team conducted a feasibility study that surveyed the one thousand local organizations implementing Pact's projects in Nepal and concluded that a potential market existed for credit of 350,000 women. She limited this number to those the Asia Foundation had the capacity to train in empowerment and advocacy, a total of 120,000 group members.

She was confident she could reach this number based on two facts. First, Pact was already delivering literacy training through a thousand local Nepalese NGOs, so she knew Pact had the capacity to reach scale. Second, and more importantly, she had learned something interesting about some of these groups. Members of several literacy groups had taken advantage of the regular meetings to do some financial transactions on the side. They had organized themselves into *dikutis* —a type of ROSCA common in Nepal, to which each member contributed a set amount of money each meeting, in turns taking the total collection from that meeting home with her. In

Marcia's mind, it would not be hard to add on to what the women were already doing.

Without an MFI to provide credit immediately, Marcia figured she could at least start the process and deal with loan capital later. While the groups were waiting to connect to external credit, they operated as savings groups, making loans to one another from the communal pot of weekly savings and sharing interest earned from the loans. Despite Marcia's best efforts, no MFIs came forward to bring her groups credit. She decided to continue with the plan anyway, forming more and more savings groups independent of MFIs. WEP was born.

Does It Last?

There was one nagging question about WEP, the answer to which I would not learn until years later. Since these groups operated mostly independently, would they survive without WEP's support? As it turned out, events allowed us to answer this important question. Soon after I completed my evaluation in 2000, USAID withdrew all funding from WEP to invest instead in a hydroelectric project. Within a matter of months, the groups were on their own. In addition, the entire region soon descended into political turmoil as the Terai Valley was taken over by Maoist rebels, and WEP pulled out entirely. When Lisa and I visited these groups, they had told us that if they were on their own they would continue saving and lending because the program was that important to them. Was this true?

Eight years later, Linda Mayoux, an internationally recognized expert on women's empowerment and microfinance, carried out a study to see whether the groups survived.[5] They had—a large portion, at least. Of the 6,500WEP groups in 2000, the 1,500 most promising groups had received substantial additional training in record keeping and management. The study, looking only at these better-trained groups, determined that two-thirds were still saving and lending. Most of us feared that all the groups would have collapsed. The biggest surprise, however, was that the "Sali Coulibalys" of Nepal had trained almost exactly the same number of new groups as the number of older groups that had disbanded—completely on their own initiative. The total number of savings groups had remained steady through eight years of unrest, without NGO support. On top of that, the number of members per group increased by four on average, and the size of the groups' loan funds quadrupled. The quality of the replicated groups was as high as that of the staff-trained groups. Unfortunately, we did not know the fate of the five thousand groups that received less training. For me, the test of the success of a program is whether it survives over time and becomes embedded into the fabric of how villages resolve the complex problems that beset them. WEP met that test.

India's Self-Help Groups

As the year that I spent immersed in WEP Nepal wound down in 2002, I began to share the strength of WEP's savings groups with my microfinance colleagues—a strength that existed not despite but *because* the groups were never connected to external lenders. Eventually, I recounted the WEP experience to Kim Wilson, a former coworker at Working Capital, the US-focused, peer-lending microfinance project I started in 1990 and managed for almost a decade. Kim was smiling and nodding the whole time, but when I got to the part where I planned to tell her how great an invention this was, she held up her hand. Asset-building savings groups, it seemed, were not unique after all.

Kim, it turned out, was already managing a savings group program of her own with Catholic Relief Services (CRS), as part of a mammoth, diverse, microfinance movement in India, the self-help groups (SHGs). Kim invited me to return with her to northern India to see a different manifestation of savings groups in action.

Kim and a shifting group of CRS staffers took me throughout West Bengal, Jharkhand, Bihar, Orissa, and Uttar Pradesh provinces on an informal journey to learn about CRS's work with SHGs. We often traveled all night by train, followed by bone-jarring jeep rides to the villages far away from the rail centers. We slept in parish houses where the Indian priests and nuns who served the region lived. After rice and dal dinners and long talks with the priests late into the night, we would find ourselves startled awake by church bells at five in the morning.

Unlike the orderly WEP meetings, at which we would hold detailed interviews one group at a time, hundreds of people showed up at each stop in India. We did not have the time or resources to arrange the carefully selected interview sampling of a full-scale project evaluation—how were we going to sort out the jaw-dropping prospect of interviewing an entire village? I shouted out my questions to the few people in the front who could hear me (or rather, my translator). From what we could decipher, many in the crowd were enthusiastic about their SHGs. It was a chaotic process and not scientific, but between these gatherings and a few poignant conversations with CRS's staff, local priests, and leaders of local NGOs, we learned what we needed to know.

The basic methodology of the SHG in India was remarkably similar to that of WEP groups, except that most groups did eventually link with banks to receive loans, which became a larger source of capital for their individual lending than was their own savings pool.

SHGs, I found, were trained and supported by a wide array of local organizations, and this led to substantial differences in how the groups operated. CRS supported small local NGOs to train groups. The Self Help

Group-Bank Linkages program promoted by India's National Bank for Agriculture and Rural Development (NABARD) would eventually became by far the world's largest microfinance initiative. According to *Banking on SHGs: Twenty Years On,* a recently published book by SHG expert Ajay Tankha, there were ninety-six million SHG members saving and lending in India as of 2012, a figure more than triple the outreach of all the other microfinance initiatives in India.[6] To put this in perspective, the Microcredit Summit, which tracks MFI outreach, reports that there are some two hundred million microfinance borrowers worldwide.[7]

At 1.2 billion inhabitants, the population of India exceeds that of all the countries of Africa combined, but it was not the size of India that I came to believe was the driver of the success of SHGs. The genius was decentralization. Thousands of different Indian NGOs (and now, increasingly, government agencies) trained the groups, and thousands of different banks—with a bank office for most clusters of villages—made loans to the groups. In this Self Help Group-Bank Linkages model, NGOs did what they do well: they trained people and provided supportive services. The banks did what they do well: they provided and administered loans. The members managed their groups. Both banks and NGOs varied from region to region, so the vast cultural variety in India was met with a variety of service providers.

Like WEP groups, the SHGs I came across in India were hubs of resilience for their members and their villages. One group in particular is etched in my memory. The members used their group meeting to prepare a complete, communitywide disaster response. The same day of their meeting, Vinod Parmeshwar, who later became the deputy director for Saving for Change, and I slipped down a muddy clay trail on foot to meet with a group readying for the monsoon. When we arrived, members were sewing together empty plastic bottles with tightened caps to create makeshift lifejackets, an ingenious if disquieting precaution for the coming flash floods. As rain pelted down on the thatch roof, they showed us the plan they had developed to protect their financial records inside ziplock bags stored with their grain on high ground. They had drawn up a map for an evacuation plan that included assisting elderly villagers to get to safety, too.

What I saw in India reaffirmed my belief that much more can be done at much lower cost by building on what is already in place than through the traditional, centralized microfinance model. The SHG movement in India used this strategy when it built on the services that NGOs were already providing in these communities to organize groups, and then used a well-established and dispersed rural banking system to deliver additional loan capital. In the state of Orissa, for example, a catechist described to me how he trained community members in SHGs at the same time that he performed his usual missionary work teaching people the fundamentals of Catholicism. Given the simplicity of the SHG model, a catechist could become a group trainer. It struck me here as in Nepal that these groups can be trained by volunteers and operate on their own, so long as the model is simple and the goal is to make the groups independent.

Zimbabwe Village Savings and Loan Associations

By this point, I was ready to be involved. I was asked by Oxfam America to direct its Community Finance Department in 2004. To begin, I booked a flight to Zimbabwe.[8] At Oxfam America's southern Africa regional office in Harare, local staff were already intrigued by the savings group idea because of the Village Savings and Loan Association (VSLA) program, the international NGO CARE's major savings group project in the country. CARE Norway's Moira Eknes is credited with developing the VSLA model in Niger in 1991, building on the *tontines* in West Africa, when she found herself unable to link the groups to credit or capital. In her words, she "developed the methodology together with the early groups."[9] Since then, CARE has expanded the model to thirty-seven countries with 3.7 million group members today.[10] In Zimbabwe, they called the project by the poetic Shona name, *Kapufuma Ishungo,* roughly meaning "to get wealthy you must persist."

The director of Kapufuma Ishungo, Alfred Hamadziripi, and I spent more than two weeks traveling from village to village learning everything we could about VSLAs in practice. In 2004, Zimbabwe was notorious for President Robert Mugabe's political repression and its consequences—the country's collapsing economy, hyperinflation, and food crisis—as well as for having one of the highest HIV/AIDS rates in the world. In spite of these crises, Zimbabweans remain some of the friendliest and most community-minded people I have met. Zimbabwe is a beautiful, fertile country with a temperate climate. I didn't miss the heat of Nepal and India.

I found the VSLA methodology very similar to that of the WEP groups in Nepal. Members saved small amounts each week, made loans from their savings, and shared the pool of savings plus interest at regular intervals. Volunteers commonly took it upon themselves to train new groups: it seemed the groups were so obviously successful that demand outpaced CARE's trainers, who found it efficient to focus on training volunteer trainers in addition to their own work forming groups. For these volunteer-trained groups to keep functioning without NGO staff, they needed to be fully capable of managing themselves. As we visited group after group, what struck us was that the trainers mostly left the groups alone unless they were stymied by a question. Each group had within itself the capacity to function on its own and to use what it had learned to train new groups.

It became clear to me that the impatience of women to join VSLA groups was not in spite of the spiraling financial crisis in Zimbabwe at the time, but because of it. By keeping the funds and decision-making power directly in the hands of the members, particularly over loan length and interest rates, VSLAs were incredibly adaptive to the rapidly deteriorating currency that was erasing savings accounts in mainstream banks and rendering cash kept at home worthless.

When I traveled to Zimbabwe in 2004, inflation was more than 500 percent per year and rising daily. Several years later, inflation rates grew to thousands and then tens of thousands of percent per annum. The government was routinely printing new currency denominations with more zeros tacked on to keep up with its deflating value. Inflation made investments in Zimbabwean dollars worth nothing in foreign exchange, and financial institutions were collapsing. I expected savings groups to be struggling, too. Instead, I found them thriving.

Despite hyperinflation, the VSLA groups were virtually the only functioning financial institutions in the country.[11] When inflation was only 500 percent in 2004, the groups had charged a high enough monthly interest rate to maintain something close to equilibrium, so when a loan was repaid, the value of the loan would come close to its value when it had been issued just a month earlier. Even traditional ROS-CAs, where for each meeting everyone would bring the same amount of money to be pooled and given as a lump sum to a different member each month, disbanded. The value of the payout for the last person in line would be worthless compared with the payout to the first member.

VSLA group members coped with inflation by maintaining their basic principles but adapting their group's specific savings amounts and meeting frequency. Groups changed the interest rates on their loans at each meeting. Some shortened loan lengths, as it was no longer sustainable to hold a loan more than a month. As hyperinflation peaked a few years after my study, I learned that savings group members would take out a loan, purchase something in the morning, trade it for a higher price in the afternoon, and pay back the loan by the end of the week. Other groups near the borders transacted in foreign currency. Some groups abandoned currency altogether and calculated loans and loan payments in terms of fast-moving consumer commodities such as bars of soap, cans of oil, and sacks of rice and maize. Groups accepted the Botswana *pula* and the South Africa *rand* even before the government began transacting in foreign currency. As transportation costs soared, groups used their collective purchasing power to send one person to buy in bulk, financing profitable cross-border trading.

I was struck by the inventiveness that group members employed to protect their assets, especially under conditions by which regulated institutions were unable to adapt quickly enough. With timely access to flexible loans that changed as often as the circumstances, VSLA members maintained their small businesses. The group members could better manage to buy food and other essentials without resorting to selling such productive assets as seeds, plows, animals, and even land, a process that had many of Zimbabwe's poorest spiraling into deeper poverty the next farming cycle because they had sold what they needed to farm with.

I also saw that savings groups such as VSLAs helped ease another crisis in Zimbabwe. At one meeting, I watched a woman stand up and proclaim she was HIV-positive to a mixed group of people with and without HIV. Her fellow group members cheered. The woman displayed extraordinary courage, I thought, because at the time (and to this day) there was a harsh stigma toward people who were HIV-positive, in Zimbabwe and in much of the world. At the time, before antiretroviral drugs became prevalent, people died quickly from AIDS. I learned that the casket maker had one of the few bustling businesses in the village.

The CARE organizers reached out to people with HIV/AIDS, initiating savings groups such as VSLAs to enable people to support themselves. The groups helped people with AIDS start trading businesses because these businesses required much less physical effort than farming, and that allowed people to still be productive even as they became sick. I watched a VSLA meeting in one village where each member contributed to a common fund so that when one of the members died of AIDS, they could have a decent funeral.

Back in Harare, Alfred Hamadziripi told me his project's story.[12] It sounded familiar. The Kapufuma Ishungo program in Zimbabwe began in 1999 and quickly trained 272 groups, with the promise that the groups would soon be linked to a matching fund. To Alfred's dismay, as soon as the first groups received their loans, they stopped saving and meeting and eventually defaulted. CARE scrapped its matching fund program and three-quarters of the groups immediately disbanded; the groups that were left were reeling and disappointed, hoping that a grant was eventually headed their way. The CARE staff revamped their program, this time with the requirement that each group would mobilize its own savings fund for loans and there would be no external capital. Starting with the handful of groups still functioning, Kapufuma Ishungo spread across the country, urged on by the wild success of savings groups to navigate hyperinflation. It turned out to be as true in Nepal and India as in Zimbabwe: the fundamental principle was to keep it simple, and no handouts.

Based on the success of CARE's VSLA project in Zimbabwe and the presence of the CARE team to provide training, we decided to start Oxfam's first savings group program in Zimbabwe. We enlisted the Zimbabwe Adult Learner's Association (ZALA) to start a VSLA-type program, pairing the savings groups with their literacy work as Marcia Odell did in Nepal. We gave a grant to ZALA for their work on the pilot project, but we found ourselves caught by Zimbabwe's rapid financial descent. ZALA had converted the grant money immediately into Zimbabwean dollars, so it lost its value so quickly that once staff were trained, no funds were left for implementation. Oxfam's—and my—first savings group program was a disaster.

Fortunately, Oxfam let me try again.

CHAPTER 4

Getting Started with Saving for Change

With the project in Zimbabwe in tatters, my colleagues and I began scouting for other places where introducing Saving for Change would make sense. Several countries in West Africa met our criteria: those with a large portion of the population living in rural areas, high rates of rural poverty, and a tradition of using groups to manage their finances. I reached out to the Oxfam America West Africa regional office in Dakar, Senegal, to develop a savings group project there. Mamadou Biteye, the senior program officer, agreed to take the project on. He later told me it was against his better judgment, but the savings concept was so counterintuitive that it intrigued him. "I was not sure how [saving] could have such a positive impact on people," he stated dryly. "I have always thought that poor people probably need more money."[1] I flew out to meet him in Senegal.

We were offered funding from the Norway-based Strømme Foundation to launch Oxfam's savings group program in Mali.[2] Mali certainly met our criteria. At that time, in 2005, 70 percent of the population lived in rural areas and 80 percent of the labor force earned their living through agriculture and fishing.[3] We later found that 82 percent of the population where we would eventually work lived below the international poverty line of $1.25 per day.[4] Malaria was endemic. The population had tripled over the last fifty years, forcing farmers to cultivate the same land year after year, reducing crop yields.[5] An increasingly unstable climate further threatened food security—some villages experienced droughts one year and floods the next.

The Cultural Context

From the start, we made the strategic decision to focus on women. At that time, the UN Human Development Index ranked Mali fifth from last of all countries in its Gender Inequality Index.[6] More recent data indicates that in Mali, the majority of people marry in their teens and 46 percent of girls have given birth by age eighteen.[7] The average woman gives birth to six children over her lifespan, and one in twenty-two women dies in childbirth.[8] Less than one-third of women can read and write (less than that in rural areas), compared with half of Malian men.[9] Women have little access to political power: in 2013, women made up just 10 percent of Mali's parliament. [10]

At the household level, social and economic norms divide family members' roles by gender.[11] Men farm the bulk of the land, although many women are allocated plots on which to grow their own crops.

Depending on ethnicity and location, men may also earn income through animal husbandry, tailoring, butchery, fishing, or laboring for others. Increasingly, younger men may migrate outside their village for work, returning during the planting and harvesting season when their labor is required. In rural Mali, it is common for families to live in extended households headed by a patriarch with several of his younger brothers or sons, perhaps each with multiple wives and their children. Though it is a cultural expectation that no man will marry an additional wife unless he can provide equally for all his wives and children, in reality it is common for different wives and their children to experience very different economic and social circumstances. Older women may find they hold power over younger wives; conversely, they may be neglected if their husbands turn more of their attention (and income) toward the new brides. In female-headed households, women must take on greater responsibilities and may face greater hardship as they navigate single parenthood amid cultural norms that often bar women from property ownership and equal inheritance and limit the earning opportunities available to them.

As a rule, men spread at least some of their harvest across the household as a whole, providing staple foods such as millet, corn, or rice, which make up the bulk of the typical Malian diet. Women are tasked with managing their households. They cook, pound millet, weed their husbands' fields, carry water from an often distant well or stream, do the laundry, shop in the market, care for infants, and educate young children. To finance their share of the household expenses, many women harvest wood for charcoal and shea nuts to refine into shea butter (both laborious processes), cultivate produce in a garden or fields, or sell produce or prepared food in the local markets. In general, women provide the "sauce" ingredients that flavor the staple grain—growing or buying tomatoes, onions, okra, and perhaps fish or a little meat. Women generally also take care of their children's clothing, school supplies, healthcare, and other everyday expenses, often paying costs themselves. Women might take turns preparing meals for their extended family or for their husband, if he has more than one wife.

Many women manage their household finances through *tontines,* where they can save for larger purchases. They may also keep money at home or, if they are a bit more prosperous, own a few chickens or goats to sell if need be. When these reserves run out, some take loans at high rates from moneylenders, while others report begging or going hungry.[12] Regardless, most rural Malian women, as well as men, lack access to formal financial services. Delivery costs are too high and credit needs are too small to make serving these Malians profitable or sustainable.[13] Mamadou and I felt this was the group with which we wanted to work: financially experienced, independent, and savvy women who faced great challenges and who could probably benefit most from better tools to manage their finances.

The Feasibility Study

Our first step was to make sure the needs we had identified resonated with the women we wanted to reach. Mamadou and I traveled to Mali to conduct a feasibility study in mid-2004. Before launching our project, we needed to understand how our idea, crafted from studying similar projects elsewhere, would be adapted to fit the Malian context. We needed to understand the interests and priorities of the women with whom we would be working. How did they manage their money? Did they have access to sufficient credit? What type of income-generating activities were they engaged in? After learning all we could before we got there, Mamadou and I arrived in Bamako, Mali's capital. Before we traveled to Mali, Mamadou Biteye, along with Edouine François and Boubacar Diallo from Freedom from Hunger, had traveled to Niger to visit CARE's impressive savings group program, Mata Masu Dubara, which translated from Hausa means "Women on the Move." This provided Mamadou, Edouine, and Boubacar an intensive introduction to how these groups work.

We set out with local Strømme staff to a nearby village with a permanent market. With its proximity to Bamako and its central square overflowing with market women displaying goods piled on brightly colored cloths spread out on the ground, this village was a hub of economic activity that we wouldn't find everywhere. Outside Bamako and a few other hubs, the majority of Mali's cities are barely more than large towns. Most of the country is made up of small villages, often clustered within walking distance of a larger village that holds a regular market, as many sellers transport their goods by donkey cart, by bicycle, or on foot, balanced on a woman's head.

The Strømme staff, working through village leaders, had organized a group of about fifty women in a circle of chairs and benches set up under a frayed canvas roof. The staff introduced us, and after formal greetings and small talk, and with the help of a translator, Mamadou and I took it from there.

"Are any of you part of a *tontine?* " I asked the group. More than half of the women raised their hands.

"How many *tontines* are represented here?" I asked. There were five. We asked the members of each *tontine* to sit together and then asked them to explain how each group was organized.

We were surprised by how diverse they were. In two of the *tontines,* the women simply made weekly payments to a group fund, eventually redistributing the amount they had saved back to each member. According to Stuart Rutherford, a scholar on financial models of the poor, individual savers use groups such as this to "create some gentle peer pressure to help ensure the savings get made."[14]

Two other *tontines* operated like the ROSCAs, which I expected. Each member contributed a fixed amount every meeting, with a different member receiving the entire sum collected at that meeting until all had received the payout once. ROSCAs replace the risk of storing cash over time (a potential pitfall for the first type of *tontine)* with the risk that if you are last in line those ahead of you may lose the incentive to continue contributing to later payouts. Rutherford notes that saving over time, receiving rotating payouts from a group, and taking out a loan all serve the same function: the user is able to control when she has a large lump sum of cash on hand, created out of small, regular payments.[15]

The fifth *tontine* used the cash it collected to buy large cans of oil and other commodities in bulk that it could resell at a profit. This buying and selling club functioned like the other groups in that it helped its members commit to saving regular, small amounts of money that might otherwise have been spent on small purchases—an extra half-kilo of rice here or a cup of tea there—until the money accumulated into a usefully large sum. Members could make a tidy profit, though they could also lose their savings in a bad investment.

We were impressed by the variety of financial instruments used by Malian women. The three types of *tontines* were fine-tuned to fit different people's needs and comfort with risk. *Portfolios of the Poor,* a landmark book exploring the strategies poor people employ to survive on tiny sums of money, makes the point that the less money you have to work with, and the less reliable or steady your income, the less secure your ability to store cash, then the more precisely you must manage every aspect of your finances: "If you are poor, managing your money well is absolutely central to your life."[16] Income must be carefully divided among everyday needs such as food, healthcare, and education as well as investments in business and agriculture to ensure future income. All this while somehow preserving quick access to the larger sums of cash (usually under fifty dollars) necessary for coping with emergencies—emergencies that are, of course, compounded by poverty: a preventable illness, for example, can become an untreatable catastrophe if you cannot afford preventive care.[17] To make our program worthwhile, we would need to understand and build on the careful, complex financial strategies already in use.

"What's missing?" I asked the group. The response was immediate. They wanted a way to access flexible amounts of money immediately without putting their long-term savings in danger. With credit, they would have the money they needed right away but pay interest. With savings, they would pay with patience. Saving for Change, we posited, would give members access to the upfront cash they wanted in the form of short-term loans while they built assets through convenient, weekly savings. Putting aside a bit of money every week is less of a burden if members know they can take out loans when they need money. When the fund is divided at the end of the cycle, each woman would receive all that she had saved plus her share of all the interest collected. Loan interest payments would become interest returned on savings down the road. Data later proved that a 40 percent rate of return on savings was not uncommon.[18]

We explained the Saving for Change method, drawing diagrams on the ground with sticks and piling pebbles to illustrate savings and loan payments. "You would keep your own records," I remember Mamadou concluding. "You would elect your own group officers. You decide on your own rules. All the records and decisions are left with the group. You decide how much you will save each week, how much interest you will charge, and what you will do if someone misses a payment. We train you on the basic structure and offer support to make sure your groups run smoothly. What do you think?"

"When can we start?" several people responded. We had to explain that this was just a feasibility study to gauge interest and to see whether the idea would work. I explained that measuring local interest and getting feedback for a project is a crucial first step in its design. If the program did indeed launch, we would send trainers to work with them a few months later. Mamadou told them that what we had learned from talking to them that day was that many women in rural Mali already have the skills to organize groups and manage their own finances. We would add to what they already knew.

As Mamadou and I traveled back to Bamako, we talked about how member ownership would be key to success. I remembered the mantra, "Dependency is not empowering." How far could we go to avoid dependency and increase ownership? "*Tontines* have spread from village to village, from market to market, long before roads, mass communication, and NGOs showed up," I said. "How can our program spread like that?" We needed to provide groups with the tools and training that would enable them to manage themselves. Our staff would need to be teachers and grassroots organizers, not financial managers. We would need an exit strategy so that groups would have no alternative except to function on their own: the trainers could work in a region for a few years organizing independent groups and then move on to train groups in new regions.

Looking back, I am proud to say that this "in their own hands" strategy worked. After the first year of training, most groups were visited only once every quarter, some even less frequently. Six years later, we could report that 95 percent of the groups trained in the first two years were still functioning, while closer to 98 percent of the groups formed later continued to save and lend.[19]

Selecting Partners

Oxfam's policy is to build local capacity by working through local NGOs rather than by implementing a project with its own staff. We decided that we would work with Malian NGOs that had already been working in their villages for some years, as they would be more likely to continue working in those villages even after Strømme, Freedom from Hunger, and Oxfam America stopped providing support. Mamadou and I prioritized local NGOs that delivered services well and at scale—for example, those related to literacy, health, education, agriculture, human rights, and finance. Saving for Change would capitalize on those organizations' connections within their communities and their knowledge of culture, traditions, and language.

After considerable searching, we found two NGOs with substantial operations in villages where we wanted to work. Le Tonus was based outside Kati, just north of Bamako, and CAEB had its central office in Bamako.[20] Both embraced the idea of our project as an interesting additional approach that would complement their ongoing microfinance work. Little did they know that in just a few months, the number of members in their savings groups would dwarf that of their struggling MFIs.

Participatory Design and Training

Meanwhile, the project's design was underway across the Atlantic at Oxfam America's headquarters in Boston, Massachusetts, and in Davis, California, where Freedom from Hunger is based. Freedom from Hunger stands out among international NGOs for its expertise in designing engaging, empowering adult education programs that it pairs with other development initiatives, such as microfinance or health. I reached out to Freedom from Hunger knowing that its expertise in project design, implementation planning, and evaluation and its deep knowledge of the Mali context would prove invaluable, as the organization already had a strong presence in the country. Happily, they were eager to work with us, and we became three partners. Strømme provided contacts and funding for the local NGOs' implementation, while Oxfam would oversee the execution and management of the initiative. Kathleen Stack from Freedom from Hunger, along with Vinod Parmeshwar, my deputy director at Oxfam's Community Finance Department, took on the nuts and bolts of curriculum design.[21] Vinod had considerable experience developing curricula from his work at CRS in India and had worked with Freedom from Hunger there.

The curriculum design team reviewed a pile of manuals, including those from Freedom from Hunger's Credit with Education program, Pact's WEP, and India's self-help groups, and the savings group manuals developed by the now-CEO of VSL Associates, Hugh Allen, for CARE's widespread VSLA program, which had by then become the standard savings group model. While drawing heavily from the existing how-to guides, we decided to try something different. "We wanted to develop our own in-house capacity to do it ourselves," explained Vinod. With our own manual, we could create "a self-reinforcing learning loop," he said, "where we were constantly updating our manuals based on what we learned from the field, so they never got stagnant."[22] For Vinod, the process was as important as the result, a principle that would become core to every aspect of Saving for Change.

marc bavois, an expert on training savings groups, worked at Freedom from Hunger when Saving for Change was just starting. In explaining this active approach to curriculum design, he said that the ultimate goal was for each group "to have a genuine, participatory discussion to come to the group's decisions," such as the savings rate or loan conditions.[23] Organizing a group that becomes "a unique institution that is making its own decisions" requires members to engage in "genuine reflection" about their own rules, instead of just copying the interest rates or late fees that work for another group.[24] Development scholar and senior lecturer in the Department of Social and Policy Sciences at the University of Bath, Dr. Sarah White, explains that participation in design profoundly changes people's experience of a program. Participation "is both a means to empowerment and an end in itself [that] transforms people's reality and their sense of it."[25] When everyone understands how the group works and why, its mechanics become transparent and leaders become accountable to members. It is much harder for someone with wealth, education, or social status to co-opt the group's resources for his or her own, what we call "elite capture."[26]

To put the plan into action, the Saving for Change team organized a three-week workshop to train the first set of animators—the staff of our local NGO partners who would organize groups. We needed to ensure that the animators understood the participatory engagement at the heart of Saving for Change—training the animators had to follow that same practical, "learning conversation" style so that the animators too felt ownership over the core principles of the training process. The animators also functioned as a critical bridge between international funders (like us) and project managers and the poor, rural women who would eventually call the shots.[27]Animators would need to have the cultural expertise to navigate the complex internal power dynamics of their villages and groups, ensuring that everyone could understand and engage on equal terms.

As the training progressed, the trainees were sent out to put into practice the lessons they had learned the day before as they formed groups in nearby villages. This practice helped develop each animator's skills while their feedback informed the program design. "It is a principle of adult learning to be able to immediately apply the learning," explained Vinod. "So as we trained the animators, we were gathering input and making real-time adjustments."[28]

After three weeks of training in January 2005, the animators were ready to start work on their own. When I returned to evaluate the program that August, I was enormously relieved to find there were already 216 groups with five thousand members in place in just seven short months. We were ecstatic.

Introducing Saving for Change and Oral Record Keeping

Not that the work was easy. Early on, many animators found that villagers were skeptical of their efforts to organize groups. "Sometimes I faced opposition," Fatoumata Traoré, one of the first animators, reflected. "Sometimes people do not believe the information of the development program—they do not believe you are who you say you are."[29] Villagers had learned from prior experience to be wary of anyone seeking to manage their finances.

Kanimba Samake, an early member and a Saving for Change volunteer responsible for training new groups in her own village, later told us about another concern. "One of the doubts I heard from other village women," she said, "was that they were worried [that] if they would get the loan, and if they had trouble paying the loan back, that they'd be put in jail.... To convince others, I told them that Saving for Change is different from other types of [microfinance], this is our own program."[30] With Saving for Change, members manage their own money, they never turn it over to the animators or NGO, and the groups themselves assess whether a member is qualified for a loan and what fines to impose on late payments or default.

Member ownership required transparency. We soon found that the written record-keeping systems we had come up with were out of place in an environment in which few women could read. Written records were *not* transparent to the illiterate majority. Written records would concentrate power in the hands of one or two members who could read or would force groups to depend on a literate volunteer, like a member's husband. Sooner or later that person would dominate the discussions and decisions of the group.[31] I had seen how written records often slow everything down. At the low levels of literacy and numeracy found in rural Mali, ledger entries would generate a lot of waiting time and frustration in meetings while a few people struggled over computations and other members waited for results that they only partially understood.

In Nepal, Marcia Odell's WEP program handled illiteracy by building reading and writing education into a fundamental part of the project. With a higher level of literacy, written records could work. CARE's VSLA model was increasingly settling on passbook-style stamp cards to keep track of member savings amounts and loan payments, with considerable success.[32] In the regions where we worked, only half of the men could read and write, and only 28 percent of women were literate.[33] We took the bold step of scrapping paper records altogether and developed instead an oral record-keeping system based on the members' existing capacity to recall a limited number of transactions.

Vinod took the lead designing the system. "We created a series of steps that we then changed as it was implemented, and over time it solidified," Vinod continued. "The key was that everything had to be announced loud and clear and it needed a regimented process."[34] Each person would hold up her savings contribution for all to see and then put it in the cashbox. Eventually, the women started to sit in the same spot each week, leading to the buddy system—each member just needed to remember her own information and that of her neighbor, both to verify her memory and to fill in if someone was absent. Vinod boiled down the record-keeping system to five essential pieces of information: did they make the savings payments; did they owe any fines; and, if they had a loan, how much was it for, when would it be repaid, and what was this month's payment? "Five points to remember for yourself and for your neighbor."

Vinod explained that "this ensured that, if the group leader left, the group wouldn't be broken apart, because the information was extremely decentralized. It also embedded participatory group management in a way that didn't create a new elite. This is something I saw in India—that the group leaders often got extra training, leading to the creation of a new elite within the group—and we didn't want that to happen. Our groups are more resilient because they're not dependent on a leader."[35]

Different groups improvised methods to make oral record keeping work better. Animator Lamine Coulibaly explained that he saw groups keep pebbles in their cashbox to count the number of meetings that had taken place and to record the number of interest payments an individual had made on a loan.[36] A group I once visited showed me how they used shea nuts and sticks to represent loans of different sizes that had been given out, allowing the treasurer to easily keep track of both the amount of cash on hand and the portion of the group's funds that was out on loan. Animators systematically spread these new ideas to other groups so that all could benefit from the inventions and innovations.

In keeping their own records, group members gained new skills and independence. Fatoumata described what a woman had told her:

> Before Saving for Change, women in our village were not able to calculate and make differences,

> but today women are able to count money from one to one million CFA. Before Saving for Change, men didn't believe women could go or meet with microfinance [loan officers] alone because men were afraid women wouldn't understand the rules, or someone would steal from women. Now men are more confident that women can go to meetings, go meet an MFI to get a loan; men do not feel obliged to accompany them. Before they never let women go alone.[37]

As time went on, Vinod and I continued to build the framework necessary to shift the locus of power in Saving for Change away from Oxfam America's Boston headquarters and to the village groups. We set up a technical unit of our best animators and NGO supervisors, led by Paul Ahouissoussi as regional program coordinator from the Oxfam West Africa regional office in Dakar. Fatoumata Traoré, the most skilled animator from CAEB, and field coordinator Soumaila Sogoba of Le Tonus had been working directly with groups for months. Their charisma and track records made them obvious picks for the technical unit. They fully understood the method, were passionately committed to it, and had credibility and respect among the other animators. Hiring from within created an internal career ladder, allowing those who excelled room to move up. We chose the next best animator at Le Tonus to replace Soumaila as supervisor there. Although Vinod and I continued to give advice and overall direction, our role moved increasingly to implementing Saving for Change in other countries. Vinod said, "I call this the backward dance.... How do you push the responsibility more and more to the people and back out of the system?" [38]

Voluntary Replication

The technical unit and partner NGOs engaged in their own backward dance, gradually expanding the role of the animator from "trainer of groups" to "trainer of trainers." In our vision, volunteer replicating agents would take on the bulk of the work of organizing new groups. At first, we imagined a spontaneous process of inspired group members bringing the savings group idea to their families and friends, or neighbors who witnessed a group's success approaching existing groups and copying their methods, as I had seen in Nepal and India. Reports of unprompted, unlinked new groups were gratifying and exciting. I anticipated that this process of spontaneous replication would cause Saving for Change to spread virally across Mali, without need for our support.

Unfortunately, spontaneous replication, though important, proved both insufficient and inefficient. Groups would often form, but they would be poorly organized, missing key elements of the structure that had been so carefully designed to ensure transparency, participation, and ownership by all members. We felt too that the rate of replication was low compared with what we had hoped for and what we would need to reach our desired scale. Animators, we learned, sometimes stopped volunteers from forming new groups because they were not sure whether they should be encouraging replication. The animators who did encourage volunteers to train new groups did so on an ad hoc basis, but their roles were confused—who did what? Should volunteers just teach from memory based on how their own groups work, could they perhaps shadow an animator while she trains and copy her process, or were they supposed to receive specific guidance?

We were encountering the tension between maintaining a high-quality program with clear structures in place to ensure effectiveness, accountability, and transparency and our desire to leave it all in the hands of the group members. The key to resolving this tension came in the form of an interactive training process that empowered participants to feel ownership over their knowledge. A later study would prove that formal training for replicating agents resulted in greater participation in Saving for Change, and better socioeconomic outcomes such as increased livestock ownership and food security.[39]

By closely observing the group replication activity already underway, we designed a system to move from laissez-faire, spontaneous replication to the "replicating agent model," discovering that we could vastly increase the number of groups trained in the process. Working closely with Freedom from Hunger, we simplified the Saving for Change manual even further, cutting text until it was almost entirely a set of simple pictures that illustrated each step in training a group. Our intent was that someone with low or no literacy skills, once trained on this manual, would have the tools to facilitate the participatory, discussion-based training sessions we felt were essential to creating member-managed savings groups.

Next, we adjusted the animator's role in introducing Saving for Change to a village. Animators would train the first group and then move on after identifying one or two smart, energetic women who wanted to take on the replicating agent (RA) role in their village. By working at the same time in twenty or more villages in an area, animators could train many RAs at once. The adventurous women willing to join a village's very first group would provide a good source of ambitious local volunteers who would then train more groups in their own villages. When the animator eventually pulled out to form groups in a new region, the RAs would continue the work independently. The endgame was geographical saturation—every village in a geographic area would have a Saving for Change group.[40] This would help ensure that even the poorest or most marginalized households in a village would be able to participate in Saving for Change.

Animator Basenji Coulibaly explained how he chose RAs from the women with whom he worked. "My criteria are that when I go to a village, I start working with a group. I try to notice and identify women who are open-minded and dedicated to the work, and whom the other women listen to. When I notice someone like that, I go to her and propose to her to become an RA. If she agrees, we go to her husband to seek his agreement before moving forward. After that, when everyone agrees (the lady and her husband), then we go ahead and I explain and teach how to create a group. 'What are the rules? What are the steps?'"[41]

Another animator, Lamine Coulibaly, reflected on the differences between paid animators and voluntary RAs. "Maybe the RA is more advantageous because she is in the village. The fact that she's always in the village [means] she knows the realities in the village.... She is living within the community so she knows the problems, speaks the same language, and speaks about the same things, so communication is better between them."[42]

A volunteer replicating agent, Fatoumata Bagayoga, explained the value of her work:

> I told them about the roles of officers and that they have to put these [positions] in place in order to become operational. I explained how they save, how they give loans, how fines and repayment are done. I talked to them about all these rules so they could understand.... Before people understood how it worked, it was challenging. I do this training even if I'm busy with my own household work. I still do the

trainings. It is important to me because of how people will consider me in the village—other people will see it is me who is doing this important role in my village....

There were some women in the village who didn't know anything about selling things or petty trading. But when Saving for Change came, and some women started small businesses, these women learned from them. The health situation of the people has also improved because it made money available to buy healthcare. This was not possible in the past because you could not get money from anybody to pay for healthcare. Another thing is if you have a child who is in school, and you have problems regarding school fees, you can borrow some money from the group and solve this problem....

I take loans from my group to buy rice, cook it, and sell it. Also I use part of the money to buy and sell shoes. I was doing this before Saving for Change. Before Saving for Change, the quantity of rice was 3kg, but now I can buy 10–15kg to cook and sell. Before Saving for Change, I sold 19,000CFA worth of shoes, but now I do 50,000CFA. Before Saving for Change, I managed with the little amount of money I could get from agriculture. It was not enough money, I was really barely managing. I bought some sheep with my share-out—five sheep for myself.[43]

CHAPTER 5

The Most Productive Asset of All: Empowering Friends and Neighbors

A savings group is a special kind of group, with a clear, indisputable purpose to fulfill an obvious, practical need. Savings groups encourage regular, continuing participation, and in doing so offer participants membership in a social club and the chance to engage in collective action. The practical nature of Saving for Change can become an excuse, a reason, to gather and work together.

In many ways, Saving for Change was perfectly adapted to fit the culture of rural Mali. There, many women already organize themselves in *tontine* groups to manage their money. Collective projects such as village gardens or work parties organized to share labor on each other's fields are common. What would happen if instead of capitalizing on a culture in which collective action and women's groups are commonplace and strong, we used the ability of Saving for Change to create social solidarity as an end goal?

In Central America, we brought Saving for Change to communities where trust had been torn by decades of violence from civil war, drug trafficking, and gangs, and where social norms meant that many women remained cloistered in their homes. The pull of regular meetings could, in certain circumstances, become even more important than the underlying motive of financial management. Even in these instances, the usefulness of a safe place to save and the draw of credit continued to motivate and justify those meetings. We saw both the outcome and the mechanism work together to improve people's lives. In Central America, we began an experiment in places where a lack of social solidarity itself was a major challenge.

El Salvador

I was excited to bring Saving for Change to Latin America. I had spent my Peace Corps service working with small farmers in Ecuador as they advocated for land rights, and I had later worked with Acción International to develop microfinance in the region. Bringing savings groups to Latin America also gave me a chance to see how the model would thrive in El Salvador, where I had first learned about microfinance twenty-five years earlier. We began with a feasibility study in Chalatenango at the invitation of the Oxfam America regional office in El Salvador.

We were drawn to El Salvador for several reasons. One was the high rate of both poverty and income inequality. In terms of income, El Salvador is one of the most unequal countries in Latin America and the Caribbean.[1] The wealthiest 20 percent of the population controls almost half of the country's wealth, while the poorest 20 percent controls just 6 percent of wealth. Within El Salvador, Chalatenango is one of the poorest regions. Half of the population lives below the poverty line, and while one in five children nationwide suffers from malnutrition, in the poorest provinces, like Chalatenango, the rate doubles to 40 percent.[2] Chalatenango was heavily affected by El Salvador's civil war and its border with Honduras became a main site of refugee movement. We branded Saving for Change as Ahorro Comunitario (Community Savings) and selected Chalatenango as the place we would start.

LAUNCHING SAVING FOR CHANGE IN CHALATENANGO

We began in Chalatenango, as always, with a feasibility study to explain the concept, gauge interest, and perhaps modify the model to fit local needs. As we explained Saving for Change to various groups of women, they listened politely and then calmly explained to us that they were too poor to save. In the words of one woman, how could they save when they "do not see a dollar all week?"[3] The first question Malian participants asked us was, "When can you start?" In Chalatenango, each woman we spoke with told us that she was not interested. We proposed to launch Saving for Change in an area where it was seemingly not feasible.

El Salvador had no savings or ROSCA tradition such as the *tontines* in Mali.[4] Some of the resistance to the idea of saving money was rooted in the economic structure in Chalatenango, where cash is not the most important form of income. The vast majority of Chalatenango's families worked on small family farms raising corn and beans, supplemented by remittances from relatives working abroad and a few small businesses—making tamales or the ubiquitous Salvadorian treat *pupusas* (tortillas stuffed with cheese).

Our interviewees, all of them women, also told us that they were afraid. El Salvador has the second highest murder rate in the world.[5] So prevalent are violence and crime that women suggested that by pooling money they would be putting not just their savings, but also their lives, at risk.[6] They were skeptical of the idea of collecting all their money in one place, even if the Saving for Change model encouraged loaning that money right back out.

Despite the negative feedback, some promising organizations were interested in launching Ahorro Comunitario: Association of Communities for Development in Chalatenango (Coordinadora de Comunidades para el Desarrollo de Chalatenango, CCR) and Caritas.[7] CCR is a member-run community organization pairing political mobilization with service delivery, with programs ranging from environmental advocacy to providing water and electricity.[8] CCR is the largest organization in Chalatenango. It has a small headquarters office, with several decentralized member-elected boards of directors and volunteer-led committees acting in each community, representing groups or issues related to youth, women, education, and culture, among others. Caritas is the social ministry of the Catholic Church, mandated with carrying out the church's mission to promote social and environmental justice.[9] Both organizations were enthusiastic about the participatory process of Saving for Change and agreed on the need for a savings and loan program in a region where reliance on subsistence agriculture leaves many families without enough liquid cash to meet daily needs throughout the year.[10]

Given the enthusiasm of these strong local organizations, my own pull toward the region, and the availability of funding, we decided to launch a small pilot project to test the program in this challenging context. Oxfam America's program officer, Milagro Maravilla, took on the role of coordinating Saving for Change in El Salvador. If you know a bit of Spanish, you know that Milagro Maravilla's name translates into English as "marvelous miracle." It seemed we would need such a miracle to be successful in Chalatenango. Luckily, we had one.

Cecilia (Ceci) Ramírez of Caritas and Esperanza Ortega from CCR were hired by Milagro to become the first *promotoras* (trainers). Both were respected leaders in their communities for many years. Cecilia's background was in teaching adult literacy skills, and even though she had only a ninth-grade education, she wanted to share what she knew.[11] Meanwhile, as a young woman during the civil war, Esperanza of CCR had returned from a refugee camp in Honduras to join the guerillas in El Salvador, and ever since then she had remained committed to struggling for social justice for her community.[12] Once Esperanza and Ceci had organized and trained a few groups—with great effort—that initial success was sufficient to secure more funding, and another ten *promotoras* were hired.

Oxfam America hired Carmen Fabian Guardado to oversee the project. In her early forties at the time she joined Saving for Change, she too came from a postwar organizing background, having joined CCR as a teenager to help resettle refugees after the civil war. Despite her experience working with local community members, she found that promoting Saving for Change was a challenge. She told me the following story, which encapsulates how difficult it was to launch the program:

> I went with Ceci to a community called Pacayas, and we were happy because thirty women showed up at the meeting.... As we presented the program, we noticed that the women were leaving one by one. Finally, there were only a few women left and Ceci began to laugh, and I told her that we could still work with them. Then she told me

> that those few remaining women were there to close up the church.[13]

Women complained that Saving for Change offered nothing but training, when most NGOs donated free services or goods. They raised concerns that this project might be a scam (of which they had seen plenty before) or that members would not pay back their loans and that the staff would steal the money. Carmen quipped "We should have had a banner that said, 'No one other than you is going to touch your money!'"[14]

Despite the initial skepticism of some of the women, five years later our initial optimism that people would join these groups was warranted. Today in El Salvador there are more than four hundred groups in place with 8,584 members.[15] Groups that were saving little are now saving much more, and some groups are lending out every penny in their group fund. The leaders of some groups are training new groups on their own. Even when funding for the team of twelve *promotoras* ended after three years, according to Milagro, "The *promotoras* continued supporting the groups that they had trained earlier as volunteers."[16] Today, the president of CCR is one of the former *promotoras* of Saving for Change. While we saw a quick launch of Saving for Change in Mali, it took five years of intensive work, and double or triple the investment per group, to launch the program in Chalatenango. The same outcome, but it took longer.

THE PROMOTORAS

Much of the success of Saving for Change in El Salvador can be attributed to these *promotoras,* who saw something worthwhile in the method and persisted in organizing savings groups despite conditions that would make most people give up. Carmen told me, "What you read in a report does not represent even one quarter of the sweat and blood it took to reach those numbers. It is very easy to trivialize what was accomplished if you do not know what it cost to organize the women, to convince them to join, and to ensure that the groups did not fall apart." I learned a lot from the *promotoras* of Chalatenango. I learned that you cannot be half-committed to do something, and that commitment takes a lot of work. The groups are delicate, and with only a single misunderstanding they can fail.

In 2013, I returned to Chalatenango to interview the staff and volunteer *promotoras* of Caritas and CCR to better understand why the program had met so much resistance in its early phases and to ask what it was that caused the *promotoras* to continue with such dogged persistence to organize savings groups. What I found was a group of women who had survived the extremes of poverty, *machismo,* and conflict. Many of these narratives of hardship coexisted alongside empowering stories of grassroots (and, in some cases, guerilla) organizing. Milagro explained that she sought out experience and dedication in her staff. "What made the difference was that we contracted women with a high degree of commitment to their communities, women who saw this as providing a service more than a job."[17] No wonder so many continued to organize groups even when they were left on their own. Here is one of these stories. What struck me was that every *promotora* and volunteer I spoke with had been active in their communities since the age of thirteen or fourteen.

Blanca Miriam Ayala Mejía, former president of the board of CCR, summed up how Ahorro Comunitario had influenced her organization, beginning by telling me about the transformative impact of being part of the program. "Sometimes when women came to the [Saving for Change] meetings they were afraid to even move out of the house, they couldn't speak, they were embarrassed, and they were afraid.... The organizational capacity, creativity, and solidarity between women has increased. At first the men were opposed but little by little they were convinced, and some even joined groups." Then she went on to say:

> Now there are women who are part of the village councils and who are mayors. Before there was jealousy among the men of the CCR board of directors about our work with women. Now this problem of jealousy has been resolved. They are not the women they were before, who would only vote for men to be the directors. Now we elect a man and we also elect a woman, and this helps the women think and participate.... If you focus

> on what this organization does, women are the ones getting things moving and doing everything.... There are empowered groups that will not fall apart easily. Saving for Change has created solidarity among women, and this strengthens the groups. CCR's support is important because with CCR's support the groups can go beyond savings.[18]

SAVING FOR CHANGE IN EL SALVADOR TODAY

It is clear that the organizers at CCR view savings groups as a means to achieve much more than economic gains for the groups' members. They emphasize, however, that meeting material needs is a crucial foundation for further empowerment. Ana Margarita Alvarenga, the Caritas *promotora,* told me how different women use the groups to manage their household finances and earnings. Although most of the groups started saving very little and were afraid to make loans, some groups, such as the one Ana Margarita describes, have evolved into substantial mini-financial organizations. This is how she describes her group today, which was organized five years earlier:

> Some of the members buy fishing nets wholesale and resell them; they sell propane gas to earn more. There are many demands for credit. Many

> carry out their business as a group to sell things like tamales, pastries, or bread. With the extra training they received, some women have gardens.... Some women have used their loans to go to school and for healthcare to buy medicines. The largest loan in our group was $600 for one month to help a member's husband buy cattle to sell. With the profits, they are building a house. Often there is no money to lend out and up to now we have never had a bad experience.
>
> Another group is making loans from $200 to $1,500. Small loans are for selling clothing, propane, and fishing nets. Some people are saving from $20 to $30 every meeting.... There are also groups that carry out small economic activities to earn money for the group fund like selling lunches. We do $0.25 to $1 raffles in the group, with the profits going to build the group fund. With just savings, the group fund does not grow very fast. For those not getting remittances, it is hard to save even $2.[19]

Of course, even these practical matters do not get in the way of organizing. "At times when we are meeting, we are not only talking about the group but about problems in the community," Ana Margarita continued. "For example, ADESCO [Asociación de Desarrollo Communal, Association for Community Development] has started to help someone in the community who doesn't have a house, and we as a group are going to see how we can help, and we are taking it upon ourselves to help the community carry out a project."[20]

Sonia Aleman, on the Saving for Change technical team for CCR, described how Saving for Change has allowed members and their communities to better weather the global financial crisis, which reduced the availability of credit to poor farmers:

> As the economic crisis deepens, the women are seeing their groups as an alternative. They don't have the documentation that the government requires for its loan funds, so they are using their groups that their communities already have as an alternative. The women are lending to their husbands for agriculture. These loans charge less interest and are less bureaucratic, and no guarantees—the house, the land—are required. The problem is that our land and our houses are in the names of our husbands and we can't get loans from the bank, so women are taking the initiative.[21]

Saving for Change created a base upon which CCR was able to expand its political strategy. Sonia explained:

> We organized the groups into networks. Each group elected one representative. All the groups in a village became a network whose representatives met together every month to share

> what they had accomplished and the difficulties that they faced. Now we have nineteen networks of groups. In these meetings the women think about what they can do beyond savings and lending. We also train the new leaders of the groups because they restructure the leadership of the groups after they close the cycles, rotating leadership roles amongst different women so more can gain this valuable experience.
>
> We are creating women's associations, and these groups are starting to establish relationships with the municipal government through formal, legal recognition, in order to be able to move beyond just being an informal network. This will force the municipalities to do what they are already required to do, given that they now have a Women's Unit and a budget earmarked for supporting women's organizational activities. We need to put on pressure because providing this assistance to women is now not something that they are going to do because they are good people, but because it is a law that they have to follow.[22]

Saving for Change provided a tool to accomplish a larger goal: grassroots political organizing. Carmen's passion shines when she explains this key concept. "Empowering women doesn't come out of nothing," she told me. "It doesn't come out of ideas; it needs to respond to the concrete material conditions of the women. I believe that this is the key."[23] She continued:

> Despite the handout mentality, individualism, and negative factors such as consumerism, there is always the possibility for change, and to a large degree, I think we were able to break this handout mentality as we built the power of these women. Politics is linked to economics. For them, making a small decision such as deciding when to meet made them realize that they could build power from their organization.
>
> Some started reaching out and visiting the mayor's office. Yes, the objective was financial, but the groups opened the political dimension. That is to say, you can't have empowerment if you have nothing. Once you resolve the material question, empowerment is nothing magical. The savings groups built empowerment, and that enabled them to see possibilities."[24]

Guatemala

The example of Guatemala helps us better understand the processes at work that made what is a financial project at the surface level into a grassroots political-organizing tool in El Salvador. We brought Saving for Change to Guatemala in early 2010.[25] Guatemala, like El Salvador, has high rates of rural poverty and an economy wracked by centuries of inequality. The two countries, like the rest of Central America, share similar histories, having been dominated by extractive industries, beginning with Spanish colonialism in the 1500s onward to the banana republic plantation economies that thrived in the 1950s. Today, Guatemala is economically the most unequal country in Latin America and among the most unequal countries in the world.[26]

As in El Salvador, the history of exploitation in Guatemala was paralleled by one of organized resistance movements by indigenous people, *campesino* farmers, urban poor, and plantation day laborers. In the 1970s and 1980s, diverse leftist guerilla movements and the right-wing owning class (including the military, political, and business elite) across Central America became proxies for the wider Cold War between the Soviet Union and the United States, receiving military training, arms, and aid. The proxy wars, tied to international-level political maneuvering, enabled the localized conflicts, fueled by deep personal hatreds, racism, and greed.[27]

Meanwhile, international economic processes over the last thirty-five years also helped maintain the structural inequalities that have long characterized Guatemalan society. Today, Guatemala has the highest rate of malnutrition in Latin America and the fourth highest rate of chronic malnutrition in the world,[28] rates comparable to a desert country like Mali. About half the children in Guatemala are undernourished (including 80 percent of indigenous children),[29] even as Guatemala's main export products are foodstuffs: coffee, sugar, bananas, vegetables, and ethanol (made from corn).[30]

Oxfam chose to introduce Saving for Change in the regions of Alta Verapaz and Baja Verapaz in central Guatemala, where large indigenous populations overlapped with high rates of poverty and women's illiteracy and where few other international development organizations already worked.[31] Alta and Baja Verapaz are also in the middle of the drug-smuggling corridor.

There was another major pull for choosing to launch Saving for Change in these neighboring central regions. Both regions were home to many experienced grassroots community organizers and existing women's committees.[32] We would be working not only in an area with great need, but one full of people already engaged in the sort of locally owned and locally managed development that Saving for Change embodies. We knew from our experience in El Salvador that if we could engage the strengths of women organizers who already embraced an empowerment methodology, then Saving for Change would reach far more women—and it would offer the organizers a useful financial tool with which to increase participation in their broader economic and social justice repertoire. This was a great way for us to support that work without directly intervening in or directing it.

SAVING FOR CHANGE AND WOMEN'S EMPOWERMENT

A few months after the launch of Saving for Change in Guatemala, we carried out a study in Alta Verapaz and Baja Verapaz to establish a baseline against which we could measure change. One key finding was that while economic indicators such as wealth were the same between those who chose to join groups and those who did not, "women who join Saving for Change groups appear to be more empowered than nonmembers."[33] Women who choose to join Saving for Change tend to be more socially active, to be less likely to need permission from a partner or father to visit friends outside their village, to participate in community or church groups, and to have more experience managing finances (saving or borrowing).[34]

Everywhere we worked required an incredible effort to get the first group going. Not until the first group of risk-taking savers got their money back at share-out were others willing to join.

Angélica Mazariegos, supervisor of the Association of Community Health Services (Asociación de Servicios Comunitarios de Salud, ASECSA), explained, "There were a lot of women in these communities, but when it was time to sign up, only a few were interested."[35] In Guatemala, this hesitation to join showed a healthy skepticism of outsider interventions that was nurtured by past experiences with failed or false projects.

In Guatemala, we found another barrier to group participation: husbands. Many men there prohibited their wives from participating in women's collective action and even threatened them with violence.

Supervisor Eleazar Timotea Castro of the Teaching Institute for Sustainable Development (Instituto de Enseñanza para el Desarrollo Sostenible, IEPADES), one of Oxfam America's NGO partners in Guatemala, told the story of how a whole group united around one woman whose husband forbade her to participate in Saving for Change:

> About six months ago a woman from Chujomil had issues with her husband, even though her husband was in the US. He would tell her that she didn't need to be part of a group. She would send the savings without telling her husband, but he still pressured her, he had control over her from afar. She eventually could not take it anymore and told the group that she could not continue because of her husband and because her in-laws had control over her as well, and that's why she was leaving the group. But the women were supportive and helped nurture a different vision of what was happening. They told her that the group is an opportunity and that her husband doesn't know all the problems we have resolved as a group because he doesn't always send you

money on time. [She] cried and cried. [36] She would not stop crying. The whole group went to her in-laws to explain what the group was, but [she] left. [She] cried because she wanted to participate.

Her friends encouraged her to have the courage to tell her husband that she has the right to participate and that the group is an opportunity. [She] and her children talked on the phone. Now her husband sends her money to save. She is good with the group and thankful of the other women who gave her the courage and the support to resolve the problem. We have a lot of cases like this one.[37]

This story did not take place in a vacuum. In a comprehensive review of studies of gender-based violence in Guatemala, Karen Musalo, director of the California-based Center for Gender and Refugee Studies (CGRS), demonstrates that Guatemala today is undergoing a crisis.[38] Musalo concludes, "Violence against women has become 'normalized' in Guatemala and is broadly accepted despite the efforts of human rights and women's groups to overcome this widespread acquiescence." [39]

In a rural area where women are generally confined to their homes and expected to follow their husbands' direction on basic financial decisions, a group like Saving for Change may be quite radical. Women's groups, which allow members space to make decisions and act for themselves, can be sites of safety, support, and resistance to this status quo. Saving for Change creates a materially useful reason for women to leave the household and meet and socialize with other women.

The *promotoras* and volunteers who work with Saving for Change know and act on this—they use Saving for Change as a tool to organize women in their communities. "The money, the savings, is a hook to get everyone organized," says Carmelina Chocooj, the Oxfam America program officer in Alta Verapaz.[40] "In general terms, the program is really important to poor women and the communities. This is the only way of keeping the women organized. In Guatemala, there hasn't been a project that can keep the women together like the savings program." Carmelina shared how in her experience, savings groups can become platforms for members to advocate on one another's behalf. "Now the women show solidarity to other women who are victims of domestic abuse, they bring them to court or have conflict resolution and accountability processes in their community."

Angélica Mazariegos, a supervisor with ASECSA in Baja Verapaz, explained how training volunteers is an opportunity to strengthen women's leadership in each community. "I see the volunteers as engines in the community, collectively teaching the methodology, and that's why we've focused on increasing the capacity that they have, because we know that [the volunteer] is going to stay in the community and keep the groups alive."[41]

Participation in Saving for Change has given members the ability to assert their human rights. Before Saving for Change, said Elena Garzón,[42] a volunteer from Baja Verapaz, "women were discriminated against. We were overlooked. They told us, 'You can't participate because you're a woman.'" She emphasized the importance of the savings group as a safe space. "Now we have that liberty to participate, to express ourselves, to value ourselves as women and somewhere to seek shelter when we have been physically or mentally mistreated.... The people say: 'It is true that we have rights, but since we do not know [what they are] we let ourselves be hurt and taken advantage of.' But now if a husband hits his wife, he goes to prison."[43]

THE CONDEMAV ELECTION SLATE

In Guatemala, a very special political victory was born out of the organizing around Saving for Change. Carmelina Chocooj was working for the Rigoberta Menchú Foundation on human rights in 2007 when she founded a community organization to focus on indigenous people's rights. Her organization, the Confederation of Women of Alta Verapaz (Confederación de Mujeres de Alta Verapaz, CONDEMAV), decided to partner with Oxfam America's Saving for Change program in Guatemala in 2011.

Carmelina attended a training in Chalatenango, El Salvador, and from there, she and the local Saving for Change team she hired managed to organize every single woman in her village into savings groups.[44]

Once she brought all the women in her village together, they mobilized their collective strength into a voting bloc.

Then they took it one step further:

> There was a community assembly in which the community authority said a new authority would be elected in fifteen days. So the women from the savings groups organized themselves and proposed a ballot with a woman candidate to be Mayor. [Our] other candidates ended up being another woman, a man, and one more woman. It was an inclusive ballot, but the women were going to hold key positions. They called this ballot "The Star."
>
> So there were three ballots: a ballot of the outgoing authority, a ballot from the men in the community, and one from the women of the savings groups.... That Sunday came and we were all nervous, worried because it was our first experience trying to take power. The voting hour came. They all went and voted.
>
> When they counted the votes, 95 percent of the votes were for the inclusive ballot—the women

> from the savings groups won! Now these women were part of the community authority. This, to me, is the biggest success we have had in Guatemala and more specifically in Alta Verapaz, within the communities of Tipulcán....
>
> After two months, we had elections at a regional level. There are fifteen to twenty communities [in the region]. Now [our candidate] is the mayor at a higher level, twenty-eight communities. She has [support from] savings groups and continues to win, so she is the mayor of the community and the region.[45]

The Star slate of candidates won 90 percent of the vote in the local election.[46] CONDEMAV's victory demonstrates the power of organizing: once women have a reason to get together, they can act together. In this community, organized women were able to take on an entire political system. The useful nature of Saving for Change makes it a particularly good tool for engaging women despite a culture of masculinity that discourages women's public participation.

Catalina Hernández[47] is a survivor of domestic violence and poverty and an outspoken advocate on behalf of indigenous people's land rights and environmental justice in the face of mining corporations. She joined a Saving for Change group in 2011, was elected president of her group, and then volunteered to train more savings groups, helping to form about twenty-five of them. Catalina united all the savings groups in her community into a women's network. She sums up the transformative power of feminist organizing through Saving for Change:

> The thing is that there are a lot of men who do not let [women] participate.... The men are opposed to it because they say the women are going to go learn how to give them orders and tell them what to do. They believe they have to tell us what to do. The fear that they have is that the women will wake up and say that the men can no longer give them orders. That's what they say in some cases [but] in others, there are men who have finally understood that saving is good, and they are doing it too. The situation has gotten better.
>
> Now some of the women say that they do not have to obey the men.... Now [men and women] can be in communication, be at home and share the work.

Although all the savings groups in El Salvador and Guatemala took full advantage of the financial benefits afforded by Saving for Change to pursue small business ventures and to smooth irregular income, many of the groups were able to use the savings groups for much more than saving and lending. In Central America, Saving for Change became a platform for broader community organizing and empowerment around important social and political issues.

CHAPTER 6

How Do We Know It Works?

It was early 2008. By this time, I had heard many stories from people in Mali, Cambodia, El Salvador, and Guatemala about how Saving for Change had changed their lives. From their stories, it was becoming increasingly clear that savings groups made a difference in their ability to save to buy food between planting and the harvest, to be resilient in the face of droughts and unplanned emergencies, and to increase their sense of empowerment.

From the perspective of a government official, international donor organization, or investor, however, it is important not only to hear these stories but to see concrete evidence showing by how much a program has affected a community. Providing answers to this question helps decision makers understand the significance of a program such as Saving for Change, and with good results helps to continue support and funding for such initiatives. Given my career conducting evaluations of other organizations' international projects, I was eager to examine Saving for Change from this perspective. My staff and I wanted to understand the impact of the groups as thoroughly as possible to make the program stronger.

I wanted to learn whether what I believed was happening was borne out by the facts.

To do this, we set up two systems: one for monitoring and another for evaluation. Monitoring allowed us to track group performance on the basis of a set of simple data points, such as number of members, amounts saved and borrowed, loan repayment and outreach, and whether groups continue to save or disband. This would enable the staff to track the spread of the program and how much it cost. Evaluation asked the "so what" questions: Did those who joined groups change how they saved and borrowed? Did their businesses grow? Did their income increase? Did they experience less hunger? Were they more likely to send their children to school? Had their decision-making role in the household and the community changed?

The design of the evaluation started much earlier than 2008. In late 2005, a few months after the first groups in Mali were trained, I designed and launched an initial survey with the help of a Malian research organization. As I visited groups with my local staff to determine what questions to include, I started with this question: What does it mean to be wealthy? One woman's response remains with me today: "A rich person has enough to eat all year, has cattle and a plow to work the land, and at least a bed to sleep on. A poor person goes hungry, has no cattle, makes do with a hoe, and has nothing at home."[1]

Did having Saving for Change groups in a village lead to less hunger and more livestock—the measures of wealth as villagers had defined it so clearly for me before? We were about to find out.

In mid-2008, Oxfam America and Freedom from Hunger secured a major grant from the Bill & Melinda Gates Foundation to evaluate the impact of participating in Saving for Change groups in Mali and to build the program in Mali, Cambodia, and Guatemala. The grant set aside more than $1.25 million for a large-scale impact evaluation in Mali, where Saving for Change had grown most quickly.[2] The Gates Foundation's decision to investigate the impact of savings groups was made at the same time that several studies were published that were critical of MFIs for overstating the impact of their work.[3] The Gates Foundation set aside so much money for research because it wanted there to be no question about the validity of the study. If the results were positive, this would justify further investment in this alternative way to promote rural financial services.

The three-year impact evaluation of Saving for Change in Mali combined a randomized controlled trial (RCT) and an in-depth anthropological study. Economists from Innovations for Poverty Action (IPA) collected baseline data in 2009, interviewing approximately six thousand women in 500 villages where Saving for Change had not yet been introduced. Of these 500 villages, 209 were then randomly selected to receive Saving for Change ("treatment" villages) and 291 were not ("control" villages). Local NGOs then began introducing the program in the selected communities. In 2012 a follow-up survey was conducted to measure the program's impact after three years, comparing the changes in villages assigned to receive Saving for Change with changes in villages assigned as control sites.

Simultaneously, a team of anthropologists from the Bureau of Applied Research in Anthropology (BARA) at the University of Arizona brought a qualitative lens to the evaluation, conducting fewer but longer and deeper ethnographic case studies in carefully selected representative villages to explain and tease out complex dynamics. The BARA team analyzed nineteen villages, fifteen in the RCT study area and four where Saving for Change had existed since 2006. The anthropologists then tracked changes in these villages over the same three years.

Who Joins Saving for Change Groups?

IPA found that women who joined Saving for Change were generally older and better connected socially in their village, although groups that formed later included women who were more socially marginalized.[4] Importantly, while it is true that women who are slightly better off are more likely to join Saving for Change, women in the lowest third household-wealth bracket (as measured by per capita food consumption) still joined in substantial numbers:

42 percent of the top third of households join compared with 33 percent of households in the bottom third.[5] Saving for Change is reaching, on average, a third of a village's poorest women, something that usually takes special targeted programming, a costly outreach effort, and extra training or support, and even then it is rarely achieved.

My strategy since I first designed the program was that the poorest could be reached not by targeting them but by saturating the village with Saving for Change groups. If most women were part of groups, then by definition the poorest would be included. I also knew that the slightly better off would join first because the poorest couldn't take the risk that their savings might not be safe—they were living too close to the margin of survival.

Did Saving for Change Help to Save for More Food?

To best evaluate the results, it is important to understand the relationship between farming seasons and the availability of food in rural Mali. For poor farmers throughout much of the world, agriculture is driven by rainy seasons when crops are planted and dry seasons that allow mature crops to be harvested, dried, and stored. In between these two natural seasons is the "lean period" of hard work before the harvest, characterized by dwindling or empty stocks of last year's harvest and similar shortages in the local economy, which drive food prices up to unaffordable levels.[6] Unfortunately, in need of cash, many farmers are forced to sell at low prices during the peak harvest season in their area and then buy food back in the lean time – often from the same traders they sold to.[7]

Prior to the introduction of Saving for Change in the impact-evaluation area, we found that an average of 40 percent of households were food insecure. In addition, we found that after three terrible years marked by drought and political violence, the average percentage of food-insecure households in all villages had risen, but the rise was tempered in the Saving for Change villages—51 percent of households suffered food insecurity in control villages, compared with 47 percent in treatment villages. Likewise, the percentage of households suffering from chronic food insecurity (as opposed to seasonal) was also four percentage points lower (39 percent) in treatment villages than in control villages (43 percent). IPA's findings also showed that households in treatment villages were better at coping through the hungry season than households in control villages.[8]

Investing in Livestock

IPA and BARA also found evidence that Saving for Change was helping families save cash for longer periods by enabling them to invest in livestock, or "saving on the hoof." To save for larger expenditures such as weddings, major illnesses, and funerals, families must find ways to access large sums of money without the risk of keeping that cash on hand, where it might be spent on any number of other daily demands. To this end, investing in animals makes financial sense: they can be a food source, they provide labor for plowing or carting goods, they can literally reproduce and grow, and they make it easier to turn down social demands from a husband, kinsmen, or friends for small cash loans.[9] Additionally, because livestock is a traditionally accepted and time-tested method of saving, many Saving for Change members preferred keeping livestock to other forms of banking and credit.[10]

The results were positive. Households in Saving for Change villages spent, on average per year, more on livestock than households in villages without Saving for Change groups. Also, in treatment areas, livestock was valued at $120 (13 percent) more than in control villages. [11]

Coping through Hard Times

In the context of a poor, rural household in Mali, the economic benefits of Saving for Change are extremely valuable. Findings from BARA's research showed that "even marginal benefits to women experienced in [a treatment village] are tremendously appreciated..... On the one hand, it indicates that for those living on the threshold of vulnerability, even slight improvements are highly meaningful; it is therefore important not to lose sight of the lived experience of Malian women in interpreting the somewhat muted impacts of Saving for Change found in this study. The perception of women in [another treatment village] is instructive in this regard: for them, Saving for Change is seen as the only workable system that is flexible enough to sustain them in times of economic crisis, when most options become untenable, and still allow them to maximize gains in times of relative plenty."[12]

Beyond the results of the impact evaluation, people living in villages that received Saving for Change told powerful stories when they were visited by program staff of how the savings groups helped them weather the 2012 food crisis. Mamadou Biteye, who had worked closely with me to design Saving for Change in 2005, reflected on a visit to Mali during the Sahel food crisis in 2012 to assess humanitarian needs there. As part of his assessment he visited some Saving for Change groups and commented that "it was amazing to have a discussion with them because we saw that the ladies were less affected by the food crisis because they could take loans in their groups to purchase food. Because they were members of the groups, they were able to run small businesses, petty trading, or microenterprises that were actually helping them earn money in the market and meet the food needs of their families. It was amazing how these women were much more resilient than those who were not members of groups."[13]

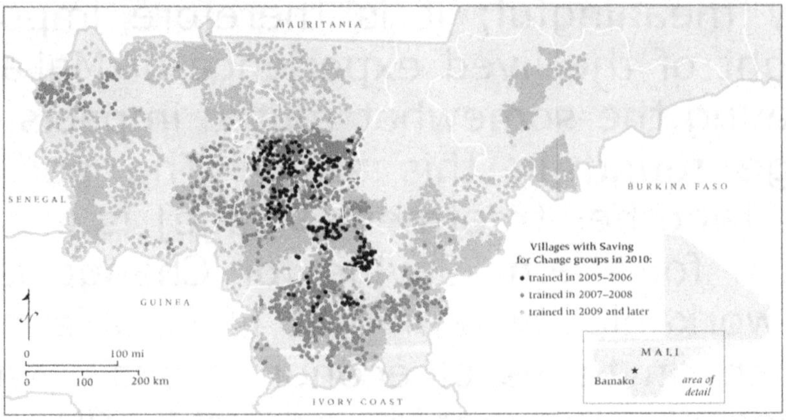

Facing page: Highlighted areas indicate the regions where savings groups were present as of 2010. Source: Oxfam America 2010

Organic Replication of Saving for Change

Voluntary replication was key to meeting our other lofty goal: scaling up. We set expectations for group formation so high that local staff had limited options: try to do everything, which was impossible, or enlist group members to train new groups. If we were to expand Saving for Change to thousands of villages in Mali, we could not do it by hiring a huge staff. Lack of resources spurred creativity. If these women members did not take the lead, then Saving for Change would not meet its objectives. The IPA researchers found that in control villages, almost one-third the number of respondents had joined a group similar to Saving for Change through replication (i.e., without a technical agent forming the group) than in the villages selected to receive Saving for

Change training.[14] This is a testimony both to the simplicity and the usefulness of this methodology. In determining the costs of introducing Saving for Change into a region, this spontaneous spread of the methodology at no additional cost should be factored in.

Limits of Impact

Despite these important, measurable accomplishments, some of the hypothesized impacts of the program were not found in the research by IPA and BARA.[15] Namely, while consumption smoothing was clearly happening—as was shown in the improvements in food security over the course of a year, the increase in the value of livestock, and the use of loans throughout the year—total income itself did not increase during the time period of the study, although it was better distributed throughout the year.[16] Saving for Change increased community-level resilience to cope with seasonal food shortages by helping members respond to shocks. However, Saving for Change in Mali had not catalyzed the long-term community transformations that our team hoped it would, such as increases in school enrollment and money spent on healthcare.[17] The timeframe of the impact evaluation may have been too short for these effects to materialize, or difficult years may have prevented these anticipated benefits from emerging. It may also be that Saving for Change does not in fact cause these desired effects.

Women's Role and Social Capital

With all our focus on participation and member ownership, we wanted to know how much power Saving for Change members really had over their groups' decisions and resources, as well as their decisions over the loans and savings they brought home. Did Saving for Change empower women in other domains outside the group itself? Did working together in savings groups give women additional respect in their villages or homes and the power to advocate for and shape their lives? Was participation worth their time—as women?

Since the earliest days of Saving for Change in Mali, participants, staff, and several studies have understood that Saving for Change can influence a deeply transformative change in members' lives. The most inconclusive results from the IPA/BARA study were the findings on decision-making power, social networks, and gender relations.

Findings from BARA's ethnographic analysis support the hypothesis that social capital increases as a result of participation in Saving for Change. Specifically, they highlighted increases in village-level solidarity and contact with other women and strengthened preexisting social ties. These findings are also consistent with prior research on Saving for Change and formal and informal interviews with countless group members that highlight how Saving for Change helps women build solidarity and confidence. However, results from the RCT do not demonstrate impacts related to social capital. The women did not expand their social networks and were no more likely to take actions, such as speaking to the chief or a government official, than they were before. While the RCT found no increase in the number of the women's contacts, the BARA anthropologists found that the depth of these relationships had increased.

How Saving for Change Changes Lives: Personal Testimonies

In the patriarchal social and political context of Mali, solidarity should also be understood as an important achievement, even if we hope to one day see Saving for Change allow women to enact more significant, transformational changes in their lives and communities by taking on larger leadership and advocacy roles. Solidarity enables women to better support each other within the choices available to them. Saving for Change, building as it does on indigenous *tontine* traditions and a participatory design, works from within Malian culture at the direction of Malian women to create accessible support systems adapted to their specific needs and circumstances right now.

Recall the passion with which some replicating agent (RA) volunteers shared their newfound status. Bassa Diakité, an RA, explained to me why she started volunteering and described the confidence and respect that came with that choice:

> I did this extra work because of the commitment I have made in front of the other women in the village. If you commit yourself to do something you have to do it. That's why I try to do everything I can. Even if I'm busy at home I manage to meet the deadline and go to the meeting.... My status changed when I became an RA because of the respect the women now have for me.[18]

In 2010, Oxfam America's senior advisor for strategic alliances, Roanne Edwards, traveled to twenty-seven villages around Mali to visit a diverse array of Saving for Change groups that were either unusually successful or unsuccessful (i.e., groups that had dissolved).[19] Among the unsuccessful groups, the overwhelming majority failed because the constraints laid out earlier became too onerous. For example, group members did not have the support of their husbands or village leaders (seen as a critical component of success), were unable to afford their weekly contributions because they were already paying off a village pump, or succumbed to interpersonal conflict between younger and older members.[20] However, to put this in perspective, these failed groups are among the less than 5 percent that disbanded; the rest are still saving and lending.[21]

Those groups that succeeded beyond expectations did so in part because they capitalized on Saving for Change's strengths. According to Edwards, "all place a premium on Saving for Change's capacity to reinforce group solidarity, elevate members' respect in their household, and offer a forum for the weekly exchange of ideas."[22] Edwards continued:

> In the village of [Fabougou], for example, one Saving for Change group successfully advocated for the building of a maternity clinic with a major donor through a local NGO. Subsequently, the nine village Saving for Change groups organized themselves into teams to pump and transport water to the construction site each day. As the president of one group remarked, belonging to Saving for Change "made it very easy to constitute the work groups because we were used to working together in Saving for Change." In the village of Banankoro, groups have worked closely with the village chief to gain access to government-run agricultural programs and to invest in a dynamo to provide electricity to the village for a small fee.[23]

Some of the groups take on projects that will have lasting impacts on gender dynamics for generations to come. For many families in Mali, birth certificates are expensive and therefore usually purchased only for boys. With a birth certificate, girls would also have documentation of their age, reducing the incidence of child marriage and labor and increasing their ability to succeed in school; without one, students may not be allowed to take exams. One Saving for Change village in particular took up the responsibility of acquiring birth certificates for all children of the members of the Saving for Change group, an initiative that required frequent negotiations with their husbands and the village chief.[24]

Several Saving for Change groups have also taken on the responsibility to train their children to save for things like school fees, generally with small allowances provided by their parents or occasionally by earning income through commercial activities such as making and selling soap. The main benefits of these children's groups are their role in teaching important financial management skills and providing an extra safety net for the family as one additional savings and loan method in a household's diverse portfolio. For some households, the savings, which could cover school fees, allowed mothers to make a case for their daughters to go to school.[25]

Fatoumata Traoré, the former animator who now sits as lead trainer on the technical unit team in Mali, shares another story of women gaining a voice in village-wide decision making through Saving for Change:

> One day a development project came to this village to get men and women to identify needs. During the meeting, men refused to invite women.

> But thanks to the Saving for Change group, all the women were able to be mobilized to choose one woman to go to represent women in this meeting. [Beforehand], everybody discussed their needs as women in this village. After the Saving for Change meeting, they stayed to discuss: we need a garden, we need water. They identified some needs and identified a woman to go to this meeting and discuss with [the development agency]. During this meeting, the chief refused to let the woman into the meetinghouse, but this woman resisted, and eventually the chief accepted and let her tell the project agent the problems of women in the village. The agent said the woman's suggestions were the best in the meeting. So after this, and for every meeting in the village, the chief wanted that one woman to be there to represent women's discussions and decisions. Before Saving for Change, the women were not mobilizing together, but thanks to the savings group, they have a communication space.[26]

Fatoumata believes strongly in the empowering potential of Saving for Change and insists that it is absolutely necessary that poor women take control of their own development. She tells groups she is training:

> The financial partners in development in the world are tired of giving money at this time because money is not enough. There are too many

> problems in the world for them to give you money, so now it is time for you to mobilize your own fund. Even if the development partner wants to help you, they are more attracted to a group that mobilizes its own fund. If someone starts to build a house, it is easy to help them finalize it, but if you have another person who hasn't started to build, she has nothing to build with, it is very difficult to help this person. It is important to build something with your own resources and capacities. If someone later wants to help you, it will be very easy for them to help you. But you need to start to build something before another can help.[27]

To Conclude

In Mali, recall that personal wealth is defined as more food and more animals. Villages where Saving for Change was introduced were less likely to be chronically food insecure and their families increased the value of their livestock and savings. The impact evaluation also indicated that substantial numbers of the poorest—those who were in the bottom third in terms of food consumption—had joined groups in substantial numbers, although those who were better off were more likely to join. Reaching the poorest was one of the objectives of the program. Although the evidence for women's empowerment was inconclusive, and RCT data showed no impact on community engagement or social networks, the anthropologists identified a strengthening of preexisting social ties. Finally, there was strong evidence of the viral, word-of-mouth replication of savings groups in the control villages, further evidence of the relevance and importance of participation in savings groups for members.

In addition to the results from the scientific-impact evaluation conducted by IPA and BARA, the anecdotal observations offered by Mamadou Biteye, Fatoumata Traoré, and Roanne Edwards indicate further change in at least some older groups, and their stories help provide a glimpse of the powerful ways that savings groups in Mali have been able to empower women in rural communities to pursue development on their own terms.

CHAPTER 7

Applying Savings Group Principles to Other Development Initiatives

A lifetime in development has taught me that the only practical way to serve the poor at a scale that makes a difference is to tap villagers' organizational acumen and aspirations for a better life. The skills that have enabled these villagers to survive exploitation, drought, and political adversity have been honed over centuries. In the face of uncertainty, their survival has always been "in their own hands." The fight for survival goes beyond geographic areas and religions. Savings groups have been promoted with equal success across Muslim Africa, Buddhist Asia, and Catholic Latin America because the prudent management of financial resources is a universal need. This chapter shows that the principles underpinning successful savings groups—relevancy, simplicity, extraordinarily low cost, local control, no giveaways, and viral replication—can be applied across the development spectrum. Interventions in education, agricultural development, public health, business education, political advocacy, conflict resolution, and women's empowerment can be designed to reflect these principles. Hope is power.

Applying Development Principles

International development practitioners can help communities take development into their own hands in many different types of programs by incorporating the high performance characteristics used for savings groups. Adherence to the principles introduced in chapter 1 will greatly increase the odds of long-term success, whatever the type of intervention.

One example of using these principles is Brazil's Cistern Program, which catalyzes the problem-solving capacity of rural communities to address the lack of water in the semiarid region of the country, which suffers from severe water shortages, with highly irregular rainfall throughout the year.[1] In response, the Brazilian government has spent billions of dollars to divert the São Francisco River to supply farmers with water, but the result has been to take water away from smallholder farmers and direct it to cities and large agribusinesses.[2]

Smallholder farmers and civil society groups in the northwest semiarid region realized that it was up to them to come up with a workable solution. In 1999, they banded together to form the Brazilian Semiarid Association and devised a plan that was simple, easy to scale, low cost, and driven by the community. Members of the association took it upon themselves to teach community members how to build different kinds of cisterns and better conserve water. The Brazilian Semiarid Association later partnered with the federal government to receive additional funding, and within a decade more than fourteen thousand people had been trained in how to build cisterns, and more than four hundred thousand families had cisterns to provide water for their small farms.[3] The top-down approach for addressing water scarcity in this region failed to reach those who needed it most. When the initiative was "in their hands" and led by those who would directly benefit, it achieved its goal.

Savings Groups as Platforms for Innovation

Just as these principles can be used to design a variety of community-based development projects, savings groups themselves can serve as effective platforms for development and empowerment initiatives. Communities have added smallholder agriculture in Central America and Zimbabwe, malaria education in Mali, HIV/AIDS education and literacy programs in Nepal, and other issues of importance as determined by members of local savings groups.[4] Building on the financial clout and social capital of savings groups, these groups find it comparatively easy to address other community-wide issues.

For example, in 2006, Freedom from Hunger launched its Microfinance and Health Protection Program, in which women who participate in savings groups discuss relevant health issues like breastfeeding, family planning, and child nutrition in addition to learning wealth-management skills. In India, the program goes beyond health education to provide access to preventative healthcare. If a doctor detects a problem, the women have access to health loans, health savings, and health microinsurance to help pay for the treatment.[5]

In Uganda, the Aga Khan Foundation has used savings groups as platforms to market solar lighting, which for rural communities has various health and cost benefits compared with traditional kerosene lamps.[6] Just as these villages are too rural for traditional financial institutions, they are often too rural to be part of a formal power grid. The program uses the savings groups' knowledge and elevated status in local communities to provide a simple solution to a widespread problem.

Another example of using savings groups as a platform for other types of development is a soil-fertility program that I helped introduce in Mali. In 2011, I contacted Roland Bunch, who built his reputation by rebuilding exhausted soils in Honduras and Guatemala,[7] and asked him to come to Mali. He had recently turned his attention from soil rehabilitation for small-scale rural farmers in Central America to Africa. Collapsing soil fertility is not just a problem for Mali—Bunch explained that "the entire lowland, drought-prone area of Africa's Sahel region is poised on the edge of severe hunger, even famine"—but the impact of this impending crisis can be lessened if soil fertility is restored for small-scale farmers.[8]

Over a few days, Bunch and I developed an agricultural intervention that built on the Saving for Change groups already in place. It was, like the savings groups, scalable, simple, locally controlled, and self-replicating. Each aspect of the design reflected the principles that made savings groups successful:

- **A vision of scale and self-replication** This was a project not only for a handful of villages but for the entire Sahel. By encouraging the spread of ideas through peer exchanges, what was learned in one hundred villages will serve as a learning laboratory to bring these services to thousands of villages over the next years.
- **Less is more, and the simpler the better** The project built soil fertility by introducing plants and trees that nourish the soil and require minimum labor. It was simple enough that it could be introduced by trainers who are not agronomists.
- **Build on what is already in place** The project used skills and tools that community members already had, such as knowledge of intercropping. The focus was on growing food for subsistence because, as once stated by John Ambler while at Oxfam America, "the first market is the stomach."

- **Be sustainable** The project introduced techniques that did not require purchased inputs such as seeds or inorganic fertilizer.
- **Keep costs low** No specialized tools, chemical fertilizers, or other agricultural inputs were required for the project.
- **No giveaways** Even seeds needed to be purchased.
- **Insist on local control** Roland introduced the program through women's Saving for Change groups and then got out of the way.
- **Establish high performance standards and insist on meeting these standards** Each animator was assigned a cluster of villages and held accountable for their performance.
- **Embrace learning and innovation** We included constant evaluation as a part of the project, with an eye to building to scale and disseminating outcomes. Also, turning over complete control to the groups allows them to adapt the program over time to better fit their needs.

This initiative with smallholder farmers in Mali addressed several issues: It helped rebuild soil fertility, provide food and fodder, increase agricultural production, and raise the water table by helping to have more water percolate into the soil. As the trees were trimmed so that they did not provide too much shade, the cuttings also provided firewood for cooking.

These outcomes may seem small to higher-income urban dwellers in the global North. However, for subsistence farmers in poor, rural societies, these improvements not only increase their incomes but also help preserve their livelihoods for the next generation and make them significantly more resilient to shocks from conflict, climate change, and drought.

While projects aimed at increasing financial inclusion and improving soil fertility may seem to have little in common, both savings groups and this agricultural intervention worked from the same basic development principles. The savings group was used as a platform to organize community members to address a pressing problem felt not just by them but the entire region.

The organic spread of good ideas is the most efficient, sustainable way to create change in any sector. As I have said throughout my work, "They know how." The same way traditional ROSCAs spread throughout villages, peer-to-peer networks have been effective at spreading knowledge on how to treat fevers, to make soap, to exclusively breastfeed, to take antiretroviral drugs for combating HIV, and to intercrop to boost agricultural productivity.

Empowering individuals and communities to take development into their own hands is the most efficient and effective way to create large-scale, durable change in the poorest and most remote communities in the world. Using this model for savings groups, I have seen the positive effects spread far beyond financial inclusion.

CONCLUSION

Bringing Savings Groups to Fifty Million People

I have been working in international development for almost half a century. I started in my twenties, bringing village leaders together in Ecuador to define how they were to secure their land under the agrarian reform law. In my thirties, I introduced solidarity group lending to Acción, leading to the commercialization of microfinance. In my forties, I brought group lending to the United States through a domestic microfinance program, Working Capital. Recognizing that microfinance would not reach the poor in significant numbers, over the past thirteen years I have embraced savings groups as the simplest and most practical way to serve the poor.

In all these endeavors, the underlying theme has been the same—providing a simple structure to help people take charge of their future. I have been both amazed and humbled by the energy and commitment of those we serve when they are in charge and we get out of their way.

The savings group experience gives us room to hope that the seemingly intractable problems of poverty can be addressed on a scale that makes a difference.

I am by no means suggesting that savings groups are sufficient for development. Access to rule of law, institutional financial services, basic services, education, roads, and markets are all necessary—but savings groups are perhaps the best and most practical place to begin.

In all my life's work, I have found that people have a common desire to join together to support one another in gaining more control over their lives. There is one truth that has been consistent—development must be "in their own hands."

In their book, *The Business Solution to Poverty: Designing Products and Services for Three Billion New Customers,* authors Paul Polak and Mal Warwick suggest, "To meet the biggest challenge in development—scale—your enterprise must aim to transform the lives of 5 million customers in the first five years and 100 million during the first ten."[9] Savings group initiatives increased their outreach from one million to ten million members in just six years.

The remarkable difference with savings groups is in how they are able to achieve this growth—not through building financial institutions as microfinance and credit unions have done or by producing and selling "relentlessly affordable" products, as Polak and Warwick suggest, but by catalyzing the problem-solving capacity of the poor. Practitioner organizations provide the simple savings group structure and transitory support. The members do the work of choosing members, electing officers, writing bylaws, mobilizing their group's fund, and issuing and collecting on loans; they take it on themselves to spread the message of savings groups within their own and neighboring villages.

Villagers join savings groups because they make their lives better. Beyond providing essential financial services that increase community resilience and reduce the effects of shocks, these groups are beginning to serve as platforms for a variety of community and economic development programs. Some groups will initiate their own projects or reach out to the government and international and local NGOs for help in building wells, schools, health posts, and roads, and the effects of the groups are being multiplied as the leaders of established groups train new ones.

Given the instability and weak institutions of the poorest countries, the fact that these groups have proved to be extraordinarily robust is yet another reason for supporting their expansion. In Mali, despite a coup, an insurgency in the north, a severe drought, an influx of refugees, skyrocketing food prices, limited opportunities for work outside the village, and faltering institutions, few Saving for Change groups have disbanded, while many new groups have been trained by volunteers.[10] Similarly, groups in Zimbabwe survived hyperinflation,[11] and groups in Nepal thrived after the withdrawal of outside support and a Maoist takeover of the region.[12] This is a testament to the power of local ownership and control that underpins the savings group approach. Savings groups cannot solve all households' problems, but villagers generally join these groups because they work. In a separate study of savings groups programs across Oxfam America, Freedom from Hunger, CARE, and CRS, researchers found:[13]

- 89 percent of the groups were still saving and lending.
- The total assets of each group—savings, interest, fines—more than doubled.
- 85 percent of the groups' funds were on loan to members.
- When the fund was divided, each member received an equivalent of $1.38 for every dollar the member saved. Instead of paying interest to financial institutions or moneylenders, they had paid themselves.

The same study showed that self-replication is occurring at staggering rates. For every staff-trained group, two more groups were established by copying what they had seen other groups do or with the help of leaders from established groups. Word-of-mouth replication had effectively reduced the cost of training a group from $400 to $133, with this cost poised to decline even further as volunteers train more groups in the years to come.[14]

Evidence from savings group programs in Uganda,[15] Zanzibar,[16] Nepal,[17] Ecuador,[18] and

Guatemala[19] documents a similar pattern of viral replication. This should not be surprising; ROSCAs—whether they are called *tontines, Susus, merry-go-rounds, tandas,* or *chit funds* —spread from village to village before roads and mass communication, and certainly before development workers like us.

Expanding Outreach to Fifty Million Group Members

At the SG 2013 savings group conference in March 2013, in Washington, DC, the major savings group practitioners—Oxfam America, Freedom from Hunger, CARE, CRS, Plan International, and the Aga Khan Foundation—presented their "50 million by 2020" vision statement.[20] The advisory committee concluded that savings groups had the potential to become a major source, if not the major source, for financial inclusion in the world's poorest countries. On reaching the target of fifty million members, savings groups will be saving and distributing more than one billion dollars ($500 per group) *of their own money* every year. The majority of those who benefit will be those living on less than $2 per day, with a majority living on less than a dollar per day. This population has been nearly impossible to reach with any level of success through traditional financial institutions, except in densely populated Bangladesh, India, and Indonesia.

The cost of growing savings groups to fifty million members is modest indeed:

- $1,000 to $1,500 per village
- $5 million to introduce savings groups to three thousand villages with a quarter of a million members
- $150 million per year over seven years to meet the fifty million group member target

The cost for training a group is trending downward. Jong-Hyon Shin, a student of mine from Brandeis University working in the Dominican Republic, is able to train savings groups through single two-hour simulations.[21] CRS is expanding its Private Sector Provider model, which pays local agents by the groups they train, further reducing the cost of expanding the program.[22] Freedom from Hunger is using low-cost mobile phones loaded with animated pictorial guides to help volunteers train groups and provide business education, which lessens costs as well. Simple applications are being tested to automate record keeping,[23] and in high-crime slums, members send their savings to the group treasurer via cell phone and groups send their extra cash to banks for safe keeping electronically.[24]

With the simple model described in this book, groups are trained quickly and operate well on their own. When we add complexity—matching funds, elaborate record keeping, or handouts—we unwittingly create dependency and undercut word-of-mouth replication, the essence of "in their own hands" development.

The stakes are high. Development has been a failure in large part, with hundreds of billions of dollars misspent. We throw the driver in the back seat and take over. Staff-intensive and costly interventions, will never serve more than a small percentage of the truly poor—that is, if they work at all. By promoting simple ideas—savings groups are only one of them—we can, to use Oxfam's term, "right the wrong."

The strategy of savings groups is based on awareness that good ideas spread as they always have: through talking with neighbors and helping one another. We will judge ourselves successful when development passes from our hands to theirs. Few will be lifted out of poverty, but the harshness of living on the edge will have been lessened, and that in itself is a major achievement. As I observe savings groups, I wonder what lessons the gaggle of children intently observing each meeting absorb as they watch their mothers undertake the revolutionary act of taking charge of their future.

Notes

Introduction

[1] OECD, "Aid disbursements to countries and regions."

[2] Rutherford and Arora, *The Poor and Their Money,* 41–42.

[3] US CIA, *The World Factbook.*

[4] Allen, "Savings Groups Global Outreach."

[5] Vinod Parmeshwar, who was to become my deputy director and who took the lead on developing the systems that ensured that the program ran smoothly, and Mamadou Biteye, who was then in charge of Oxfam America's programming in West Africa and who was later to direct the regional office for West Africa for Oxfam America and later Oxfam Great Britain. Kathleen Stack along with Edouine François of Freedom from Hunger, Vinod, and Mamadou trained the local staff. Freedom from Hunger and Oxfam jointly developed the training manuals and training protocols.

[6] Coulibaly, "Saving for Change."

[7] Salimata Coulibaly interview.

Chapter 2

[1] "Solidarity, or *benkadi,* is a widespread term used in Mali (and by far the most common name chosen by Savings groups)." BARA and IPA, *Final Impact Evaluation,* 119. *Benkadi* directly translates to "togetherness is sweet."

[2] Approximate currency conversions from 2012–13.

[3] "Oral accounting has been a successful mechanism to assure transparency for all members, and allows for financial management by the group even when more complex systems such as multiple shares are introduced." BARA and IPA, *Baseline Study of Saving for Change in Mali,* 15.

[4] Several sources discuss this contrasting aspect of emergency loans. They are not private, because members must ask their group for money. However, they are more discreet (and reliable) than begging or asking family, and many members value this aspect of Saving for Change very highly. See, for example, Bermudez and Matuszeski, *Ensuring Continued Success,* 15–16.

[5] BARA and IPA, *Baseline Study of Saving for Change in Mali,* 86.

[6] "Women perceive Saving for Change as a buffer against shock. Loans are occasionally used for

consumption emergencies and emergency loans are in fact prioritized by the group and in many cases are repaid without interest." BARA, *Operational Evaluation of Saving for Change in Mali,* vii.

[7] "For many women, the mere presence of a program that validates their economic struggles and establishes a buffer against risk is enough in itself to motivate them toward savings and credit where previous systems did not." BARA and IPA, *Baseline Study of Saving for Change in Mali,* 16.

[8] "Most households of any type will run out of the most important staples (millet, sorghum and rice) at some point during the year." BARA and IPA, *Baseline Study of Saving for Change in Mali,* 64.

[9] "Husbands of members also assist members with loan reimbursement under certain conditions, such as sickness or business failure, that disable a member from repaying her debt." BARA, *Operational Evaluation of Saving for Change in Mali,* 51.

[10] "While many women take loans for petty enterprises and commerce, they tend to co-mingle the profits. These enterprises are thus frequently decapitalized as funds are diverted to meet immediate household needs. While this leads to a pattern of repeated loans

to sustain the same activity, such activities rarely grow under these conditions. Even in areas where Saving for Change has had a longstanding presence, women are by and large taking out loans for the same activities as when they began the program. The few women we observed who have been able to realize transformative economic growth through Saving for Change enjoyed relative wealth and stability before the program arrived." BARA and IPA, *Baseline Study of Saving for Change in Mali,* 89.

[11] Description of the animator's role and the training program drawn from Parmeshwar interview and Freedom from Hunger and Oxfam America, *Saving for Change Formation of Savings Groups: Animator's Guide.*

[12] BARA and IPA, *Final Impact Evaluation,* 13.

[13] "The two keys to group *survival* are women's *confidence* in themselves and in the group, and their *willingness* to make things work. Confidence comes from knowing Saving for Change content; having a capable individual—committee member or RA—to guide the group; and/or experiencing an extended period without animator visits.... Women's willingness to make things work reflects their motivation, optimism and excitement about the

program." Bermudez and Matuszeski, *Ensuring Continued Success,* 6 (emphasis in original).

[14] US Global Health Initiative, "Mali."

[15] The process for identifying and training replicators is drawn from interviews with animators and replicating agents, February 7–8, 2013, in Kebila and Faragouran, Mali.

Chapter 3

[1] United States Agency for International Development (USAID), the US government's bilateral aid agency.

[2] Ashe and Parrott, *Pact's* WEP *in Nepal,* 6.

[3] Achyut Hari Aryal interview.

[4] Roodman, *Due Diligence,* 119. This ratio refers to group solidarity lending models. For all types of microfinance, the staff-to-loan ratio ranges from 238 staff per individual loan to 306 staff per "village banking" style loan.

[5] Mayoux, *Women Ending Poverty.*

[6] Tankha, *Banking on SHGs,* 35; Srinivasan, *Microfinance India,* 3.

[7] Maes and Reed, *State of the Microcredit Campaign Report 2012,* 3.

[8] Nageeb Sumar assisted with this project.

[9] Helmore, "Revisiting the Early Days of CARE's Savings Groups," 61.

[10] Allen, "Savings Groups Global Outreach."

[11] Hamadziripi interview.

[12] Ibid.

Chapter 4

[1] Biteye interview.

[2] For more information on the Strømme Foundation, see http://Strommestiftelsen.no/english.

[3] Romana, "Saving for Change in Mali."

[4] BARA and IPA, *Final Impact Evaluation,* 59.

[5] Howard, "Mali's 2.5 Percent Problem."

[6] UNDP, "GII: Gender Inequality Index, value."

[7] UNICEF, "Mali Statistics."

[8] Ibid.

[9] UNDP Mali, "Promouvoir l'égalité des sexes."

[10] IPU, "Women in National Parliaments."

[11] The gendered division of labor and financial roles in Mali is well documented. See, for example, Creevey, *Women Farmers in Africa.*

[12] BARA and IPA, *Baseline Study of Saving for Change in Mali,* 77.

[13] Romana, "Saving for Change in Mali."

[14] Rutherford and Arora, *The Poor and Their Money,* 39, 2.

[15] Ibid., 12.

[16] Collins et al, *Portfolios of the Poor,* 4.

[17] Ibid., 174–5.

[18] BARA and IPA, *Final Impact Evaluation,* 11.

[19] Ruberg, *Saving for Change in Mali,* 20.

[20] The acronym CAEB stands for Conseil et Appui pour l'Éducation à la Base in French, meaning "Counsel and Advice for Education for All."

[21] Kathleen Stack took the lead for Freedom from Hunger, along with Susan Grove, a graduate student from the microfinance course I taught at Columbia University.

[22] Parmeshwar interview.

[23] bavois interview.

[24] Ibid.

[25] White, "Depoliticizing Development," 61.

[26] There was a tension between the need for skilled facilitators with the capacity to tease

input and ideas out of their trainees and the ultimate goal of making training itself so accessible and easy that group members would feel empowered to train new groups. The solution was counterintuitive: we needed to lay out a fully scripted, participatory dialogue, said marc bavois. "We give people a formula [that] replaces the capacity of the trainer to actually facilitate." The Saving for Change manual would walk trainers through each step of leading an active discussion, question by question, prompt by prompt. A standardized learning conversation would ensure that every training created space for diversity and experimentation in each group: inexperienced trainers could copy this dialogue instead of copying a rigid set of group rules. From bavois interview.

[27] Dunford, "Field Agents Matter, Too."

[28] Parmeshwar interview.

[29] Traoré interview.

[30] Samake interview.

[31] Salimata Coulibaly interview.

[32] Hugh Allen, the CEO of VSL Associates, a consortium of savings group practitioners, continues to help craft the VSLA model. He shared with me a fascinating commentary on written records: with passbooks, he said, "It occurred to me that ledgers are an intellectual

construct in which facts are translated into an abstract form so that results can be calculated. But most poor people have enough confidence in the system that they do not need to be reassured by a constant (and usually inaccurate) re-calculation. Passbooks are very concrete and visual, with their stamps, which is somehow closer to the way in which people in villages construct reality. What they see and hear is more powerful than what is rendered only abstract as a set of results. So passbooks work everywhere except when there are very low levels of literacy.... In Mali the oral system has broken the mold for an illiterate target group." Allen interview.

[33] BARA and IPA, *Baseline Study of Saving for Change in Mali,* 39.

[34] Parmeshwar interview.

[35] Ibid.

[36] Lamine Coulibaly interview.

[37] Traoré interview.

[38] Parmeshwar interview.

[39] BARA and IPA, *Final Impact Evaluation,* 61–62.

[40] Oxfam America, "Saving for Change FY14 Outlook," 1.

[41] Basenji Coulibaly interview.

[42] Lamine Coulibaly interview.

[43] Bagayoga interview.

Chapter 5

[1] El Salvador Country Leadership Team, *Joint Strategy of Oxfam International in El Salvador,* 5.

[2] Oslin, *Saving for Change in El Salvador,* 5; US CIA, "El Salvador"; El Salvador Country Leadership Team, *Joint Strategy of Oxfam International in El Salvador,* 8.

[3] Sostowski and Maravilla, *Estudio de Factibilidad,* 23.

[4] Ibid., 11.

[5] UNODC, "UNODC Homicide Statistics."

[6] Sostowski and Maravilla, *Estudio de Factibilidad,* 5.

[7] In Spanish, CCR is known as the Coordinadora de Comunidades para el Desarrollo de Chalatenango. The acronym is derived from its former name, the Comité Coordinador para las Reptriaciones, which reflects the organization's original mandate to protect the rights of returning formerly displaced people and rebuilding the community after the civil war.

[8] Devietti and Matuszeski, *Saving for Change Program Assessment,* 19.

[9] Ibid., 20.

[10] Ibid., 11.

[11] Ibid., 207.

[12] Ibid., 176.

[13] Ibid., 150.

[14] Ibid., 151.

[15] Allen, "Savings Groups Global Outreach."

[16] Alas, *Programa de Ahorro y préstamo comunitario El Salvador y Guatemala,* 137–65.

[17] Ibid., 144.

[18] Ibid., 159–65.

[19] Ibid., 218–19.

[20] Ibid., 219.

[21] Ibid., 172–73.

[22] Ibid., 168.

[23] Ibid., 156.

[24] Ibid.

[25] Devietti et al., *Saving for Change in Guatemala Baseline,* 3.

[26] Guatemala Country Leadership Team, *Guatemala,* 3.

[27] Manz, *Paradise in Ashes,* 21.

[28] UN WFP, "Guatemala: Overview."

[29] Devietti and Harrison, *Feasibility Study Literature Review,* 2.

[30] US CIA, "Guatemala."

[31] Rodriguez, *Bringing Saving for Change to Guatemala,* 2.

[32] Ibid., 11–12.

[33] Devietti et al., *Saving for Change in Guatemala Baseline,* 25.

[34] Ibid., 23–4.

[35] Alas, *Programa de Ahorro y préstamo comunitario El Salvador y Guatemala,* 83–91.

[36] Name removed to protect identity.

[37] Alas, *Programa de Ahorro y préstamo comunitario El Salvador y Guatemala,* 35–39.

[38] Musalo, Pellegrin, and Roberts, "Crimes without Punishment."

[39] Ibid., 170.

[40] Alas, *Programa de Ahorro y préstamo comunitario El Salvador y Guatemala,* 9–21.

[41] Ibid., 83–91.

[42] Name changed to protect identity.

[43] Alas, *Programa de Ahorro y préstamo comunitario El Salvador y Guatemala,* 68–71.

[44] Ibid., 9–21.

[45] Ibid.

[46] Ashe, *Trip Report,* 5.

[47] Name changed to protect identity.

Chapter 6

[1] Ashe, *Saving for Change,* 6.

[2] Further details and in-depth analysis on the hypotheses, methodology, data, and results of the impact evaluation described in this chapter appear at length in BARA and IPA, *Final Impact Evaluation.*

[3] For a thorough literature review of impact studies on microfinance, see Roodman, *Due Diligence,* 153–71.

[4] BARA and IPA, *Final Impact Evaluation,* 113–14.

[5] Ibid., 43.

[6] Chambers, foreword to *Seasons of Hunger,* xxi.

[7] Devereux, Vaitla, and Swan, *Seasons of Hunger,* 21.

[8] BARA and IPA, *Final Impact Evaluation,* 36, 51, 52.

[9] Ibid., 92.

[10] Ibid.

[11] Ibid., 52.

[12] Ibid., 109.

[13] Biteye interview.

[14] BARA and IPA, *Final Impact Evaluation,* 15.

[15] Ibid., 112.

[16] Ibid., 112–13.

[17] Ibid.

[18] Diakité interview.

[19] Edwards, *Saving for Change in Mali,* 4.

[20] Ibid., 7.

[21] Ruberg, *Saving for Change in Mali,* 20.

[22] Edwards, *Saving for Change in Mali,* 5.

[23] Ibid.

[24] Ibid.

[25] Ibid., 41–45.

[26] Traoré interview.

[27] Ibid.

Chapter 7

[1] Bateman and Brochardt, "Brazil's Lessons in Rural Development."

[2] Ibid., 15.

[3] Ibid., 17.

[4] Rippey and Fowler, "Beyond Financial Services."

[5] Freedom from Hunger, "Microfinance and Health Protection."

[6] Rippey and Nelson. "Beyond Financial Services."

[7] Bunch, *Two Ears of Corn.*

[8] Bunch, "Africa's Soil Fertility Crisis."

[9] Polack and Warwick, *The Business Solution to Poverty,* 197.

[10] Sogoba interview.

[11] Hamadziripi interview.

[12] Mayoux, "Women Ending Poverty."

[13] Savings Groups Information Exchange.

[14] Ibid.

[15] Mine, et al., "Post-Project Replication of Savings Groups in Uganda."

[16] Anyango, et al., "Village Savings and Loan Associations."

[17] Mayoux, "Women Ending Poverty."

[18] Proaño, Gash, and Kuklewicz, "Durability of Savings Group Programmes."

[19] Alas, *Programa de Ahorro y préstamo comunitario El Salvador y Guatemala,* 118–32.

[20] Oxfam America, "International savings groups NGOs aim for 50 million members by 2020."

[21] Shin interview.

[22] The Savings and Internal Lending Communities (SILCs) program pioneered by CRS uses the Private Service Provider (PSP) model to fund up to one year of training of community agents who will continue to provide SILCs training and support at a fee after the funding from CRS, through a local implementing organization. This provides sustainability and continuity and also ensures that the services provided by the trainers address local market needs for savings and lending requirements.

[23] Rippey and Wanjau, "No More Tears."

[24] Wilson, "Jipange Sasa," 99–107.

Bibliography

Alas, Carolina Díaz. *Programa de Ahorro y préstamo comunitario El Salvador y Guatemala: Informe de Entrevistas.* Translated by the author, Julissa Cotillo, and Cristobal Lagunas. San Salvador, El Salvador: Oxfam America, 2013.

Allen, Hugh. Interview by author. Solingen, Germany, and Boston, MA (via Skype). June 15, 2012.

______. "Savings Groups Global Outreach." Accessed February 27, 2014. http://www.seepnetwork.org/savings-groups-global-outreach-pages-20015.php.

Anyango, Ezra, Ezekiel Esipisu, Lydia Opoku, Susan Johnson, Markku Malkamaki, and Chris Musoke. "Village Savings and Loan Associations: Experience from Zanzibar." *Small Enterprise Development* 18 (2007): 11–24. Accessed February 27, 2014. doi:10.3362/0957-1329.2007.004.

Ashe, Jeffrey. *Saving for Change: Initial Findings of the Baseline Survey and Future Plans for Saving for Change Initiative in Mali.* Boston, MA: Oxfam America, 2006.

______. *Trip Report: El Salvador and Guatemala.* Boston, MA: Oxfam America, 2013.

Ashe, Jeffrey, and Lisa Parrott. *Pact's* WEP *in Nepal: A Savings and Literacy Led Alternative to Financial Institution Building.* Cambridge, MA: Brandeis University and Freedom from Hunger, 2001.

Bagayoga, Fatoumata. Interview by Souleymane Sogoba. Faragouran, Mali. February 7, 2013.

Ballo, Sarata. Interview by Souleymane Sogoba. Nagalasso, Mali. February 7, 2013.

Bateman, Joseph, and Viviane Brochardt. *Brazil's Lessons in Rural Development.* Washington, DC: Washington Office on Latin America, February 2013.

bavois, marc. Interview by author. Washington, DC. March 6, 2013.

Beaman, Lori, Dean Karlan, Jonathan Morduch, and Bram Thuysbaert. "Impact Evaluation of Saving for Change Endline Survey: Preliminary Findings." Presentation at the IPA-OA-Freedom from Hunger Dissemination Workshop, Boston, MA, October 13, 2012.

Bermudez, Laura, and Janina Matuszeski. *Ensuring Continued Success: Saving for Change in Older Program Areas of Mali.* Boston, MA: Oxfam America, 2010.

Biteye, Mamadou. Interview by author. Dakar, Senegal, and Boston, MA (via Skype). February 28, 2013.

Bunch, Roland. "Africa's Soil Fertility Crisis and the Coming Famine." In *State of the World 2011: Innovations That Nourish the Planet,* 59–68. Washington, DC: Worldwatch Institute Report, 2011.

_____. *On the Saving for Change-Plus Agriculture Program in Mali.* Boston, MA: Oxfam America, 2012.

_____. *Two Ears of Corn: A Guide to People-Centered Agricultural Improvement.* Oklahoma City, OK: World Neighbors, 1995.

Bureau of Applied Research in Anthropology (BARA). *Operational Evaluation of Saving for Change in Mali.* Tucson, AZ: University of Arizona, 2008.

Bureau of Applied Research in Anthropology (BARA) and Innovations for Poverty Action (IPA). *Baseline Study of Saving for Change in Mali: Results from the Segou Expansion Zone and Existing Saving for Change Sites.* 2010.

_____. *Final Impact Evaluation of the Saving for Change Community Microfinance Program in Mali 2008–2012.* 2013.

Carter, Marion W. "Gender and Community Context: An Analysis of Husbands' Household Authority in Rural Guatemala." *Sociological Forum* 19 (2004): 633–52.

Chambers, Robert. Foreword to *Seasons of Hunger: Fighting Cycles of Quiet Starvation among the World's*

Rural Poor, by Stephen Devereux, Bapu Vaitla, and Samuel Hauenstein Swan, xvi–xix. London: Pluto Press, 2008.

Collins, Daryl, Jonathan Morduch, Stuart Rutherford, and Orlanda Ruthven. *Portfolios of the Poor: How the World's Poor Live on $2 a Day.* Princeton, NJ: Princeton University Press, 2009.

Coulibaly, Basenji. Interview by Souleymane Sogoba. Kebila, Mali. February 8, 2013.

Coulibaly, Lamine. Interview by Souleymane Sogoba. Bougouni, Mali. February 7, 2013.

Coulibaly, Salimata. "Saving for Change." Oxfam America, 2006. Video: 3 minutes, 32 seconds.

Coulibaly, Salimata. Interview by author. Mali. 2006.

Creevey, Lucy. *Women Farmers in Africa: Rural Development in Mali and the Sahel.* Syracuse, NY: Syracuse University Press, 1986.

Devereux, Stephen, Bapu Vaitla, and Samuel Hausenstein Swan. *Seasons of Hunger: Fighting Cycles of Quiet Starvation among the World's Rural Poor.* London: Pluto Press, 2008.

Devietti, Eloisa, and Gregory Harrison. *Feasibility Study Literature Review: Guatemala.* Oxfam America, 2009.

Devietti, Eloisa, and Janina Matuszeski. *Saving for Change Program Assessment.* Oxfam America, 2009.

Devietti, Eloisa, et al. *Saving for Change in Guatemala Baseline.* Oxfam America, 2011.

Diakité, Bassa. Interview by Souleymane Sogoba. Mali. February 12, 2013.

Duflo, Esther. "Grandmothers and Granddaughters: Old Age Pension and Intra-Household Allocation in South Africa." NBER Working Paper Series 8061. December 2000.

Dunford, Chris. "Field Agents Matter, Too: The Social Capital Builders." In *The Evidence Project: What We're Learning about Microfinance and World Hunger.* Last modified March 15, 2013. http://microfinanceandworldhunger.org/wordpress/2013/03/field-agents-matter-too-the-social-capital-builders/.

Edwards, Roanne. *Saving for Change in Mali: A Study of Atypical Groups from Sikasso to Kayes.* Boston, MA: Oxfam America, 2010.

El Salvador Country Leadership Team. *Joint Strategy of Oxfam International in El Salvador,* 5th Draft. El Salvador: Oxfam America, 2011.

Freedom from Hunger. "Microfinance and Health Protection." Accessed March 30, 2014. https://www.f

reedomfromhunger.org/microfinance-and-health-protection-0.

Freedom from Hunger (FFH) and Oxfam America. *Saving for Change Formation of Savings Groups: Animator's Guide.* Davis, CA, and Boston, MA: 2008.

______. *Saving for Change Formation of Savings Groups: Trainers Guide.* Davis, CA, and Boston, MA: 2008.

Garnier-Crussard, Pauline. *Saving for Change Case Studies Research in Sirakoro.* Bamako, Mali: Oxfam America, 2011.

Guatemala Country Leadership Team. *Guatemala: Análisis y Estrategia de País de Oxfam.* Guatemala: Oxfam America, 2011.

Hamadziripi, Alfred. Interview by author. Boston, MA, and Harare, Zimbabwe (via Skype). November 16, 2012.

Hari Aryal, Achyut. Interview by author. Boston, MA. November 12, 2012.

Helmore, Kristin. "Revisiting the Early Days of CARE's Savings Groups: Interview with Moira Kristin Eknes, Village Savings and Loan Associations (VSLA) Program Originator." In *Financial Promise for the Poor: How Groups Build Microsavings,* 57–68, edited by Kim

Wilson, Malcolm Harper, and Matthew Griffith. Sterling, VA: Kumarian Press, 2010.

Historical Clarification Commission [CEH]. *Guatemala: Memory of Silence.* Guatemala: 1999.

Howard, Roger. "Mali's 2.5 Percent Problem." *Foreign Policy,* January 28, 2013. Accessed May 14, 2013. http://www.foreignpolicy.com/articles/2013/01/28/mali_s_population_growth_problempercent20.

Inter-Parliamentary Union (IPU). "Women in National Parliaments." Last modified July 1, 2013. http://www.ipu.org/wmn-e/classif.htm.

La Via Campesina. *Small-Scale Sustainable Farmers Are Cooling Down the Earth.* Jakarta: 2009.

Lecocq, Baz, Gregory Mann, Bruce Whitehouse, Dida Badi, Lotte Pelckmans, Nadia Belalimat, Bruce Hall, and Wolfram Lacher. "One Hippopotamus and Eight Blind Analysts: A Multivocal Analysis of the 2012 Political Crisis in the Divided Republic of Mali: Extended Editors Cut." Last modified May 15, 2013. http://bamakobruce.files.wordpress.com/2013/04/lecocq-mann-et-alhippo-directors-cut.pdf.

Maathai, Wangari. "Nobel Lecture." Last modified December 10, 2004. http://www.nobelprize.org/nobel_prizes/peace/laureates/2004/maathai-lecture-text.html.

Maes, Jan P., and Larry R. Reed. *State of the Microcredit Campaign Report 2012.* Washington, DC: Microcredit Summit Campaign, 2012.

Manz, Beatriz. *Paradise in Ashes: A Guatemalan Journey of Courage, Terror, and Hope.* Berkeley and Los Angeles: University of California Press, 2004.

Matuszeski, Janina. *Timeframe for Hypothesized Changes.* Boston, MA: Oxfam America, 2013.

Mayoux, Linda. *Women Ending Poverty: The Worth Program in Nepal: Empowerment through Literacy, Banking, and Business 1999–2007.* Kathmandu, Nepal: Valley Research Group, 2008.

Mine, Sarah, Shawn Stokes, Marcy Lowe, and Sarah Zoubek. "Post-Project Replication of Savings Groups in Uganda." Datu Research, VSL Associates, November 7, 2013.

Musalo, Karen, Elisabeth Pellegrin, and S. Shawn Roberts. "Crimes without Punishment: Violence against Women in Guatemala." *Hasting Women's Law Journal* 21 (2010): 161–221.

Niyibizi, Glycerie et al. *Mind the Gap: Exploring the Gender Dynamics of* CARE *Rwanda's Village Savings and Loans (VSL) Programming.* Rwanda: CARE, 2012.

Organisation for Economic Co-operation and Development (OECD). "Aid disbursements to countries and regions." *Development: Key Tables from OECD,* No.5, 2012. Last modified April 4, 2012. Accessed February 23, 2014. http://www.oecdilibrary.org/development/development-key-tables-from-oecd_20743866.

Oslin, Jane Martha. *Saving for Change in El Salvador: Pilot Project Evaluation.* Oxfam America, 2007.

Oxfam America. "International savings groups NGOs aim for 50 million members by 2020." Accessed March 14 2014. http://www.oxfamamerica.org/press/international-savings-groups-ngos-aimfor-50-million-members-by-2020/.

_____. "Saving for Change FY14 Outlook: Phase 2: 'SAVING FOR CHANGE + 'Projects.'" *Saving for Change Quarterly Update* (June 2013).

_____. *Saving for Change: Financial Inclusion and Resilience for the World's Poorest People: Report Summary.* Oxfam America and Freedom from Hunger, May 2013.

Parmeshwar, Vinod. Interview with author. Boston, MA. January 11, 2013.

Pinstrup-Andersen, Per, and Derrill D. Watson Jr. *Food Policy for Developing Countries: The Role of Government in Global, National, and Local Food Systems.* Ithaca, NY: Cornell University Press, 2011.

Polack, Paul, and Mal Warwick. *The Business Solution to Poverty: Designing Products and Services for Three Billion New Customers.* San Francisco: Berrett-Koehler, 2013.

Proaño, Laura Fleischer, Megan Gash, and Amelia Kuklewicz. "Durability of savings group programmes: A decade of experience in Ecuador." *Enterprise Development and Microfinance* 22 (June 2011): 147–60. Accessed February 27, 2014, doi: 10.3362/1755-1986.2011.017.

Rippey, Paul, and Ben Fowler. *Beyond Financial Services: A Synthesis of Studies on the Integration of Savings Groups and Other Developmental Activities.* Aga Khan Foundation, April 2011.

Rippey, Paul, and Candace Nelson. *Beyond Financial Services: Marketing Solar Lamps through Savings Groups: Emerging Lessons from Uganda.* Aga Khan Foundation, April 2011.

Rippey, Paul, and Kuria Wanjau. "No More Tears." Financial Sector Deepening Kenya, *FSD Updates* 8, September 2013.

Rodriguez, Juana. *Bringing Saving for Change to Guatemala: Oxfam America's Low-Cost, Mass-Scale Financial Services for the Poorest Rural Regions.* Oxfam America, 2009.

Romana, Sophie. "Saving for Change in Mali: Too Poor Not to Save." Presentation, Boston, MA, April 30, 2013.

Roodman, David. *Due Diligence: An Impertinent Inquiry into Microfinance.* Washington, DC: Center for Global Development, 2012.

Ruberg, Lynnae E. *Saving for Change in Mali: A 2005–2010 Panel Study of Informal Savings Groups.* Waltham, MA: The Heller School of Social Policy, Brandeis University, April 25, 2011.

Rutherford, Stuart, and Sukhwinder Arora. *The Poor and Their Money: Microfinance from a Twenty-First Century Consumer's Perspective.* Warwickshire, UK: Practical Action Publishing, 2009.

Samake, Kanimba. Interview by Souleymane Sogoba. Faragouran, Mali. February 7, 2013.

Sanford, Victoria. "From Genocide to Feminicide: Impunity and Human Rights in Twenty-First Century Guatemala." *Journal of Human Rights* 7 (2008): 104–22.

Savings Group Information Exchange. VSL Associates. Accessed March 8, 2014. http://savingsgroups.com.

Shin, Jong Hyon. Interview by author. Washington, DC. March 6, 2013.

Shiva, Vandana. *Soil Not Oil: Environmental Justice in an Age of Climate Crisis.* Cambridge, MA: South End Press, 2008.

Sogoba, Soumaila. Interview by author. Boston, MA. September 19, 2012.

Sostowski, Aimee, and Milagro Maravilla. *Estudio de Factibilidad para el Desarrollo de un Programa de Ahorro y Prestamo en El Salvador.* Oxfam America, 2006.

Srinivasan, S. *Microfinance India: State of the Sector Report 2012.* New Delhi: Sage Publications India, 2012.

Tankha, Ajay. *Banking on SHGs: Twenty Years On.* Thousand Oaks, CA: SAGE Publications, 2012.

Traoré, Fatoumata. Interview by author. Bamako, Mali, and Boston, MA (via Skype). January 23, 2013.

UNICEF. "Mali Statistics." Last modified February 26, 2003. http://www.unicef.org/infobycountry/mali_statistics.html.

United Nations Development Program (UNDP). "GII: Gender Inequality Index, Value." *Human Development Indicators.* Last modified October 12, 2012. https://data.undp.org/dataset/GII-Gender-Inequality-Index-value/bh77-rzbn.

United Nations Development Program (UNDP) Mali. "Promouvoir l'égalité des sexes." Last modified 2013. http://www.ml.undp.org/content/mali/fr/home/mdgoverview/overview/mdg3.

United Nations Office on Drugs and Crime (UNODC). "UNODC Homicide Statistics." Last modified 2013. http://www.unodc.org/unodc/en/data-and-analysis/homicide.html.

United Nations World Food Program (UN WFP). "Guatemala: Overview." Accessed June 14, 2013. http://www.wfp.org/countries/guatemala/overview.

United States Institute for Peace. "Truth Commission: Guatemala." Accessed June 14, 2013. http://www.usip.org/publications/truthcommission-guatemala.

US Central Intelligence Agency (US CIA). "El Salvador." *The World Factbook.* Last modified May 15, 2013. https://www.cia.gov/library/publications/the-world-factbook/geos/es.html.

_____. "Guatemala." *The World Factbook.* Last modified August 13, 2013. https://www.cia.gov/library/publications/the-worldfactbook/geos/gt.html.

_____. *The World Factbook.* Accessed February 25, 2014. https://www.cia.gov/library/publications/the-world-factbook/.

US Global Health Initiative. "Mali." Accessed May 1, 2013. http://www.ghi.gov/whereWeWork/profiles/Mali.html#.U3zqKepOVNA.

White, Sarah. "Depoliticizing Development: The Uses and Abuses of Participation." In *The Participation Reader,* edited by Andrea Cornwall, 57–71. London: Zed Books, 2011.

Wilson, Kim. "Jipange Sasa: A Little Heaven of Local Savings, Hot Technologies, and Formal Finance." In *Financial Promise for the* Poor, edited by Kim Wilson, Malcom Harper, and Matthew Griffith. Sterling, VA: Kumarian Press, 2010.

World Health Organization (WHO). "Mali Health Profile." Last modified May 2013. http://www.who.int/gho/countries/mli.pdf.

Additional Resources

To learn more about the organizations mentioned in *In Their Own Hands* and to continue the conversation surrounding the savings group revolution, you can find further information from the following list of resources:

Oxfam America

Oxfam America is a global organization working to right the wrongs of poverty, hunger, and injustice. As one of 17 members of the international Oxfam confederation, Oxfam America works with people in more than 90 countries to create lasting solutions. Oxfam saves lives, develops long-term solutions to poverty, and campaigns for social change.

For more information, see http://www.oxfamamerica.org/

Freedom from Hunger

Freedom from Hunger Freedom from Hunger brings innovative and sustainable self-help solutions to the fight against chronic hunger and poverty. Together with local partners, Freedom from Hunger equips families with resources they need to build futures of health, hope, and dignity.

For more information, see https://www.freedomfromhunger.org/

Strømme Foundation

The Strømme Foundation is a Norwegian international development organization that helps poor people in the global South climb out of poverty through microfinance and education.

For more information, see http://strommestiftelsen.no/english

Bill & Melinda Gates Foundation

Guided by the belief that every life has equal value, the Bill & Melinda Gates Foundation works to help all people lead healthy, productive lives. In developing countries, it focuses on improving people's health and giving them the chance to lift themselves out of hunger and extreme poverty. In the United States, it seeks to ensure that all people—especially those with the fewest resources—have access to the opportunities they need to succeed in school and life.

For more information, see http://www.gatesfoundation.org/

Bureau of Applied Research in Anthropology (BARA), College of

Social and Behavioral Sciences, University of Arizona

The Bureau of Applied Research in Anthropology (BARA) is a unique academic research unit within the School of Anthropology at the University of Arizona. BARA's mission is to place anthropology at the service of contemporary society, prepare the next generation of professional anthropologists, advance knowledge of the human condition, and address the pressing issues of local communities. BARA faculty and affiliates carry out research, teaching, and outreach activities within Arizona, throughout the country, and internationally.

For more information, see http://bara.arizona.edu/

Innovations for Poverty Action (IPA)

Innovations for Poverty Action is a nonprofit organization dedicated to discovering what works to help the world's poor. IPA designs and evaluates programs in real contexts with real people and provides hands-on assistance to bring successful programs to scale.

For more information, see http://www.poverty-action.org/

Aga Khan Foundation

The Aga Khan Foundation (AKF) focuses on a small number of specific development problems by forming intellectual and financial partnerships with organizations that share its objectives. Most of the foundation's grants are made to grassroots organizations testing innovative approaches in the field. With a small staff, a host of cooperating agencies, and thousands of volunteers, the Aga Khan Foundation reaches out to vulnerable populations on four continents, irrespective of their race, religion, political persuasion, or gender.

For specific information on the Aga Khan Foundation's work with savings groups, see http://www.akdn.org/akf_beyond_financial_services.asp

CARE

CARE is a leading humanitarian organization fighting global poverty. Women are at the heart of CARE's community-based efforts to improve basic education, end gender-based violence, provide healthcare and nutrition, increase access to clean water and sanitation, expand economic opportunity, and protect natural resources.

For specific information on CARE's work with savings groups, see http://www.care.org/work/economic-development/microfinance

Catholic Relief Services (CRS)

Founded in 1943 to service World War II survivors in Europe, CRS works to assist impoverished and disadvantaged people overseas, working in the spirit of Catholic social teaching to promote the sacredness of human life and the dignity of the human person. Although its mission is rooted in the Catholic faith, its operations serve people based solely on need, regardless of their race, religion, or ethnicity. Since 1943, CRS has expanded in size to reach more than one hundred million people in ninety-one countries on five continents.

For specific information on CRS' work with savings groups, see http://crs.org/microfinance/

The Consultative Group to Assist the Poor (CGAP)

CGAP is a global partnership of thirty-four leading organizations that seek to advance financial inclusion. CGAP develops innovative solutions through practical research and active engagement with financial service providers, policy makers, and funders to enable approaches at scale. Housed at the World Bank, CGAP combines a pragmatic approach to responsible market development with an evidence-based advocacy platform to increase access to the financial services the poor need to improve their lives.

For more information, see http://www.cgap.org/

Plan International

Plan is an international, child-centered development organization working with seventy-eight million children in fifty developing countries across the world to promote child rights and lift millions of children out of poverty.

For more information, see http://plan-international.org/

The Carsey School of Public Policy, University of New Hampshire

The Center on Social Innovation and Finance (CSIF) at the Carsey School of Public Policy at the University of New Hampshire conducts rigorous and timely research on sustainable community development and supports training and research initiatives on the impact of savings groups to increase financial inclusion for poor people and communities. Carsey has been a leader in training for savings groups practitioners, offering workshops through its Sustainable Microenterprise and Development Program (SMDP) in

Southern, East and West Africa since 2004 and co-organized the first global summit of savings groups practitioners in Arusha, Tanzania attended by more than 260 practitioners from 51 countries.

For more information, see http://carseyinstitute.unh.edu/

The Savings Group Information Exchange (SAVIX)

The SAVIX is a reporting system that provides transparent and standardized data on savings group programs worldwide. The SAVIX's goal is to facilitate analysis and improve program results by comparing regional, country, project, and trainer performance.

For more information, see http://savingsgroups.com/

Savings Revolution Blog

The Savings Revolution blog is a forum for practitioners of savings groups to develop and exchange ideas on savings groups and financial inclusion. Launched in January 2011, the site has built an online library of more than one hundred documents related to savings groups, hosted in coordination with the Savings-Led Working Group of SEEP, as well as numerous podcasts, videos, and photos.

For more information, see http://www.savings-revolution.org

The SEEP Network

The SEEP Network is a global network of more than 120 international practitioner organizations dedicated to combating poverty through promoting inclusive markets and financial systems. SEEP represents the largest and most diverse network of its kind, composed of international development organizations and global, regional, and country-level practitioner networks that promote market development and financial inclusion. Members are active in 170 countries and support nearly ninety million entrepreneurs and their families.

For more information, see http://www.seepnetwork.org/

Globalization and Sustainable Development Program

The Globalization and Sustainable Development Program at Tufts University's Global Development and Environment Institute (GDAE) carries out policy research to further just and sustainable international trade and development. Priority research areas include the global food crisis, foreign investment, China's role in Latin America, and reforming US trade policies.

178

http://www.ase.tufts.edu/gdae/policy_research/globalization.html

Acknowledgments

We must start with our admiration for the hundreds of thousands of group members, the thousands of volunteers, and the hundreds of staff whose courage, incredibly hard work, and dedication made Saving for Change a reality. The credit for the success of Saving for Change is truly "in their hands."

For Jeffrey, there are so many to thank: Marcia Odell for introducing me to savings groups in Nepal; Kim Wilson for everything I learned in India; Constance Kane, Oxfam America's director of regional programs, for hiring me in 2004 at Oxfam America and for believing in Saving for Change; Mamadou Biteye, who got Saving for Change rolling in Mali; John Ambler, Oxfam America's senior vice president for programs, for his wisdom and advocacy; Chris Dunford, Kathleen Stack, Megan Gash, Laura Fleischer-Proaño, Edouine François, and the team at Freedom from Hunger who were our partners in this venture. Roanne Edwards urged me to write this book for years before I finally did.

It was Soumaïla Sogoba, Fatoumata Traoré, and Paul Ahouissoussi who made Saving for Change a reality in Mali and Senegal through their tireless efforts; Milagro Maravilla and Carmen Fabian led the team that did the same in El Salvador and Guatemala; and Vanndeth Seng, Sampha Phon, and Socheata Sou built Saving for Change in Cambodia. In Boston, Vinod

Parmeshwar translated the Saving for Change vision into an operational reality; Eloisa Devietti conducted research, developed manuals, and kept us organized; Janina Matuszeski and Clelia Anna Mannino oversaw our ambitious research agenda; and Andrea Teebagy managed the finances. Sophie Romana is now leading Saving for Change at Oxfam America, ably assisted by Belicca Ferrer. Sophie also had a major role in reviewing this manuscript. Darius Teter, Oxfam America's current vice president for programs, has promoted Saving for Change as a priority program, and Jane Huber, Oxfam's creative director, guided us through the editorial process. Roland Bunch took the lead in making agricultural development relevant to the rural poor in Mali and El Salvador.

Dean Karlan and Jonathan Morduch at Innovations in Poverty Action, Mamadou Bara from the Bureau of Applied Research in Anthropology, and their staffs were involved for more than three years in answering the question of the impact of Saving for Change and how it works.

My savings group fellow travelers at the Carsey Institute at the University of New Hampshire—Bill Maddocks, Paul Rippey, Hugh Allen, Malcolm Harper, and Candace Nelson—have been an ongoing source of inspiration and support. Michel Swack has a major behind-the-scenes role at the Carsey Institute and played a critical role earlier in launching Working Capital. Our objective at the Carsey Institute is to grow savings group outreach from one hundred thousand to one million villages. Large thanks also go to my colleagues at the Global Development and Environment Institute at Tufts University, where I am a research fellow. At Brandeis University, where I teach in the Sustainable International Development Program, my thanks to Susan Holcombe and Larry Simon, and at Columbia, my thanks to Eugenia McGill, who has been my link to the university.

Joyce Lehman, our project officer at the Bill & Melinda Gates Foundation, showed enormous insight and flexibility as we built Saving for Change. Dorothy Largay, president and CEO of the Linked Foundation, provided the early critical support to build Saving for Change in El Salvador, and Shigeki Makino played a similar role in Cambodia.

This book would never have become a reality without Kyla Jagger Neilan, who worked with me tirelessly on this project for more than a year and who had a critical role in making this book as good as it is. Kyla and I also thank our graduate research assistants, Emily Cole, Heather LeMunyon, and Joseph Bateman, from the Fletcher School at Tufts University, who have gone above and beyond in helping us bring this story to life. Kyla and I also extend our thanks to Catherine Thomas, Leslie Puth, and Johanna Goetzel, who worked with us in the early days of writing the book. Simone LaPray from the Heller School for Social Policy at Brandeis University, has taken over the role of the previous group of assistants and is helping me on the marketing of the book.

Many thanks to Frances Moore Lappé, who graciously wrote the foreword to this book and was inspired by how she saw savings groups as an antidote to powerlessness, as well as to Ray Offenheiser, Oxfam America's president, who wrote the Preface. Additional thanks go to Steve Piersanti, the president of Berrett-Koehler Publishers, for seeing the importance of this book and advocating for it, and to Jeevan Sivasubramaniam, who led us through the editorial process. Mal Warwick not only reviewed the manuscript and introduced me to Berrett-Koehler—decades ago, he served along with me as a Peace Corps volunteer.

I am pleased that Berrett-Koehler encouraged and supported the inclusion of color pages, allowing us to tell our story through photographs I took in the field. I have photographed many extraordinary individuals and communities over the years, and am grateful they granted permission to share their faces with you, the reader.

I want to thank my children, Whitney and Katya, for putting up with their dad, although the truth is that I spent too much time rambling around the world. My wife Alyce, my children, and my granddaughters, Tatiana and Lauryn, are those who make me want to come home. Alyce has been my toughest editor and fiercest advocate.

Kyla would like to thank her partner, (the other) Jeff; her intellectual comrade in arms, Alex Shams; and for everything, Mom and Dad, Faye and Bill Neilan.

Finally, the many weeks that we spent talking to the women who took the risk of joining these groups, who told us about their lives, and explained what their savings groups have meant to them have been truly inspirational. We expect to hear much of them in the years to come.

About the Authors

Jeffrey Ashe

I've worked as a catalyst of social change for decades, and there is one lesson that continuously rings true: success happens when problem solving is "in their own hands"; failure occurs when others try to do it for them.

After graduating from UC Berkeley, I began my career in international development as one of the early Peace Corps volunteers in Ecuador. Assigned to a remote village, I developed a program in which my team of fellow volunteers and Liberation Theology nuns brought together village leaders to plan how to secure the land they were entitled to. As the village leaders brought agrarian reform to more villages, I realized that success was theirs, not mine. After leaving Ecuador and completing graduate studies in sociology at Boston University, I joined Acción International in

1975. As Acción's deputy director, I led the first worldwide assessment of microfinance, which later became the framework for launching microfinance in Latin America and later Africa and Eastern Europe. Throughout the 1980s, I evaluated, designed, and led microfinance efforts in thirty-five countries, and in 1990, I brought microfinance to the United States with Working Capital, which soon had operations in eight US states, the West Bank and Gaza Strip, and Russia. In 1997, I received the award for microfinance innovation from President Bill Clinton.

After becoming disillusioned because microfinance was not reaching the world's poorest, it was my evaluation of the Women's Empowerment Program in Nepal in 2000 that taught me that there was another path to financial inclusion. By sidestepping financial institutions and instead training small groups to save and lend, village women were being reached at an unprecedented scale. Taking what I learned in Nepal, and later in India and Zimbabwe, I joined Oxfam America in 2005 as Oxfam's director of community finance. It was there that I designed and led the Saving for Change initiative, which grew to organize more than 650,000 rural women into tens of thousands of savings groups across five countries with minimal staff and at low cost, capitalizing on their capacity to lead their own development.

Currently, as a research fellow at the Global Development and Environment Institute at Tufts University and as a fellow at the Carsey Institute at the University of New Hampshire, I am part of a group of "Savings Revolution" leaders working to bring savings groups to one million rural communities over the next decade. Through the courses I teach at Brandeis University and Columbia University, I am dedicated to inspiring the next generation of change agents. At the conferences and universities around the world where I am invited to speak, my message is that the key to change is "in their own hands."

About Kyla Jagger Neilan

Kyla Jagger Neilan is a researcher, practitioner, and activist for social justice and food sovereignty. She holds an MPA in international development from Cornell University and a BA from Oberlin College in Third World studies, with minors in environmental studies and French. Kyla is the recipient of awards for gender and environmental research and fellowships from myAgro, the Cornell Institute of Public Affairs, and the Environment Ohio Research and Policy Center. She has worked for Oxfam America, the United Nations World Food Program, Catholic Relief Services, and journalist Naomi Klein. Her research on women's and farmer's organizations, with fieldwork in Mali, Ethiopia, and Tanzania, focuses on gender and food systems at the margins, seeking to understand and be in solidarity with social movements for food sovereignty, agro-ecology, and global feminisms that address root causes of food crises, environmental racism, and gender-based violence. At home in Boston, Kyla lives in co-ops, goes to punk shows, and keeps a permaculture vegetable garden. Currently, Kyla is working with farmers in the Central African Republic to recover their livelihoods after conflict.

Over the course of more than a year, Kyla Jagger Neilan and Jeffrey Ashe worked closely together developing the majority of the book. The bulk of the research responsibilities fell to her, and in several cases she would interview Jeff before and throughout the drafting of several chapters. The collaborative process made the book stronger as Kyla helped Jeff bring his experience to the page.

OXFAM AMERICA is a global organization working to right the wrongs of poverty, hunger, and injustice. As one of 17 members of the international Oxfam confederation, we work with people in more than 90 countries to create lasting solutions. Oxfam saves lives, develops long-term solutions to poverty, and campaigns for social change.

HOW DO WE FIX THE INJUSTICE OF POVERTY?

Oxfam's approach is about tackling the conditions that cause poverty in the first place, rather than the distribution of material goods. We start by asking questions and challenging assumptions. What are the root causes of poverty? What can we do to change the power dynamics that keep people poor? These questions inform the four categories into which our work falls:

SAVING LIVES: Oxfam assists the poorest communities when disaster strikes, but is also working to ensure greater local resilience and the capacity of local responders and governments to deliver disaster response.

PROGRAMS TO OVERCOME POVERTY AND INJUSTICE: Oxfam invests in programs to help people assert their rights so that they can improve their lives.

CAMPAIGNING FOR SOCIAL JUSTICE: Oxfam works to change the laws and practices that keep people trapped in poverty.

PUBLIC EDUCATION: As part of our efforts to overcome poverty, Oxfam works to change the way people think about poverty and its causes.

To join our efforts or learn more, go to oxfamameric a.org.

Berrett–Koehler
BK Publishers

Berrett-Koehler is an independent publisher dedicated to an ambitious mission: *Creating a World That Works for All.*

We believe that to truly create a better world, action is needed at all levels—individual, organizational, and societal. At the individual level, our publications help people align their lives with their values and with their aspirations for a better world. At the organizational level, our publications promote progressive leadership and management practices, socially responsible approaches to business, and humane and effective organizations. At the societal level, our publications advance social and economic justice, shared prosperity, sustainability, and new solutions to national and global issues.

A major theme of our publications is "Opening Up New Space." Berrett-Koehler titles challenge conventional thinking, introduce new ideas, and foster positive change. Their common quest is changing the underlying beliefs, mindsets, institutions, and structures that keep generating the same cycles of problems, no matter who our leaders are or what improvement programs we adopt. We strive to practice what we preach—to operate our publishing company in line with the ideas in our books. At the core of our approach is stewardship, which we define as a deep sense of responsibility to administer the company for the benefit of all of our "stakeholder" groups: authors, customers, employees, investors, service providers, and the communities and environment around us.

We are grateful to the thousands of readers, authors, and other friends of the company who consider themselves to be part of the "BK Community." We hope that you, too, will join us in our mission.

A BK Currents Book

This book is part of our BK Currents series. BK Currents books advance social and economic justice by exploring the critical intersections between business and society. Offering a unique combination of thoughtful analysis and progressive alternatives, BK Currents books promote positive change at the national and global levels. To find out more, visit www.bkconnection.com.

Dear Reader,

Thank you for picking up this book and joining our worldwide community of Berrett-Koehler readers. We share ideas that bring positive change into people's lives, organizations, and society.

To welcome you, we'd like to offer you a free e-book. You can pick from among twelve of our bestselling books by entering the promotional code BKP92E here: http://www.bkconnection.com/welcome.

When you claim your free e-book, we'll also send you a copy of our e-newsletter, the *BK Communiqué.* Although you're free to unsubscribe, there are many benefits to sticking around. In every issue of our newsletter you'll find

- A free e-book
- Tips from famous authors
- Discounts on spotlight titles
- Hilarious insider publishing news
- A chance to win a prize for answering a riddle

Best of all, our readers tell us, "Your newsletter is the only one I actually read." So claim your gift today, and please stay in touch!

Sincerely,

Charlotte Ashlock
Steward of the BK Website

Questions? Comments? Contact me at bkcommunity@bkpub.com.

U

V

W

Z

Made in United States
North Haven, CT
05 November 2026

21766923R00141